Live on Purpose:

100 encouraging thoughts to live on purpose.

By Caleb Gaines

Day 1:

What are you waiting for? Start living on purpose!

Ecclesiastes 3:12-13 - "So I concluded there is nothing better than to be happy and enjoy ourselves as long as we can. And people should eat and drink and enjoy the fruits of their labor, for these are gifts from God"

Live today is if it is your last day, because you never know if it may be! Do what makes you happy, live out your passions, and pursue your dreams! There is nothing better than realizing that you have the potential to make today the best day of your life! Quit living for 'the day off' or for the next thing that you think will make you happy. With God first in your life you can experience true joy and vigor for life now! When you choose to start living on purpose you will stop 'waiting' for life to happen and make it happen. Enjoy the blessings and people God has given you.

Obviously, be responsible with life and worldly things, but God has placed blessings in your life for you to enjoy. You weren't created to have to endure life, but enjoy it! So today, focus on shifting your mindset and realizing that because of God today can be the best day of your life!

Lord, help me to enjoy the little things. I'm done waiting for life to happen to me and I commit to making life happen. Open my eyes to the beauty of being alive. Today is a brand new day and I will live it full of joy and passion for you!

Day 2:

To get something different, you have to do something different.

Isaiah 43:19 "Look, I am about to do something new; even now it is coming. Do you not see it Indeed, I will make a way in the wilderness, rivers in the desert."

I fully believe God is always wanting to do something new in our lives and it doesn't always look the same. God is not a God who always speaks in the same way or gives us the same 'sign' as He did last time. Sometimes we have to do something new! That may look like searching The Scriptures deeper, spending more time in prayer alone, or even getting outside your comfort zone to engage in community with other believers. If we want to get rid of the old habits, old lifestyles, and old bondages it is on us to do something different. The verse before that says to forget the former ways and do not dwell on the past.

We can't always expect God to do things the same way every time it may look different, but that is where growth comes from! God has already set 'the new' into motion now it's your job to meet Him there!

Thank you God that you are always doing something new. Give me the courage and faith to step out and do something different. I don't want to live the same way or get the same results anymore, but I want what you have for me. Thank you that your plan for me is a good plan. Today I receive the new that you have for me and the courage to do something different. Amen

Day 3:

Healthy leaders have healthy habits.

Proverbs 4:20-23 - My son, pay attention to my words; listen closely to my sayings. Don't lose sight of them; keep them within your heart. For they are life to those who find them, and health to one's whole body. Guard your heart above all else, for it is the source of life."

As Christians we are called to be leaders and healthy leaders at that. How can the world be changed if they don't see any difference between us and them? Being a healthy leader comes down to your habits. Proverbs reminds us to pay attention to our words and to keep God's commands in our heart, because they bring health to the body. It also tells us to guard our hearts above all else! If we want to be great leaders, we must first guard our hearts and our habits.

Whatever habits you currently have are a determining factor of where your heart is and where it is going. The effort to create and maintain good habits separates good leaders from great leaders. Are you eating healthy? Are you exercising enough? Do you actively spend time in God's word and in His presence? Who do you allow to speak into your life? What do you allow to speak into your life? Do you spend too much time on a screen? All of these little things play a big role in guarding our hearts and helping us become the healthy leaders God has called us to be. So today, take a moment and write out some unhealthy habits you may have and the good habits you can replace those with.

Lord, thank you that you have called me to be a healthy leader. Help me identify the bad habits in my life. I ask that you would help me find healthy ones to replace them with. You have called me to be a healthy leader I will do whatever it takes to guard my heart and become the healthy leader that you have called me to be. Amen.

Day 4:

99% isn't enough of you.

Romans 12:1 - "Therefore, brothers, by the mercies of God, I urge you to present your bodies as a living sacrifice, holy and pleasing to God; this is your spiritual worship."

God wants all of you. I don't say that just to make you feel better, but it is actually a fact from Heaven that God wants all of you. He gave all He had when He sent Jesus so that He could have all of you! Unfortunately, many times we give God 99% of our heart, our efforts, and our thoughts and think that is enough. Yes, 99% is good, but sometimes it's the 1% we won't give Him that is hindering the call of God on our lives. This scripture urges us to daily live as a sacrifice to God.

This is how we worship Him, by giving Him 100% of our sins, doubts, fears, failures, and past. God anoints a fully sacrificed life ! No, this doesn't mean you have to be perfect, but you do have to be surrendered. Today, refuse to let the 1% hold you back from your destiny!

Lord, thank you that you want all of me. Thank you that you are not content with just 99% of me, but you want all of my mess. Thank you that I can come to you with an open heart. I acknowledge that I have not been living as a daily sacrifice, but I declare that from today onwards I will live my life fully surrendered to you. I receive your love, grace, and forgiveness. Thank you for the power to overcome and move on. Amen.

Day 5:

How are reaching your community outside of church?

Matthew 5:14-15 - "You are the light of the world. A city situated on a hill cannot be hidden. No one lights a lamp and puts it under a basket, but rather on a lampstand, and it gives light for all who are in the house."

As Christians it can be so easy to get stuck in our 'church bubble,' where we hang out with the same people, sit with the same people, and invest in the same people. It can be easy to flip an on and off switch on the light of Jesus in us. A good friend of mine once emphasized that "we can never switch off." You are the light of the world! Because Jesus is in you, you have the answer to all the problems in today's world!

Now that you know you carry the answer, what are you doing to invest in others and in your community outside of the church? You have the ability to reach people your pastor, worship leader, and small group leader never even knew existed. Find ways today to engage the lost and bring the solution of Jesus to meet their needs!

God, help me to seize the day and find opportunities to invest in others outside of church. I don't want to be a 'light switch' christian and only flick on when I am in church. Help me to see the needs of others and act on it. Thank you that Jesus is the answer to all the world's problems. Amen.

Day 6:

Value your reputation with God more than your reputation with man.

John 15: 20-21 - "Remember the word I spoke to you: 'A slave is not greater than his master.' If they persecuted Me, they will also persecute you. If they kept My word, they will also keep yours. But they will do all these things to you on account of My name, because they don't know the One who sent Me."

In life you will face persecution for the name of Jesus. Whether that be physical, emotional, or whatever the case may be if you are truly living for Jesus people will slander your name. One thing I have learned is that God will always have your back. There have been times where I have been called a liar, kicked out of meeting places, had nasty things said about me, and been left out because of my faith. In those moments, God was still by my side, stronger than ever before.

I can tell you from staying faithful and valuing my reputation with Him more, those same people who before hated me, came to know who He is because of how I lived. So today, if you are fighting that battle, know God will always have your back. Today, know that the same people who are mocking and maybe even hurting you now will one day bow down at the feet of Jesus! Keep living for Him and the Lord will guide you, bless you, and anoint you for your faithfulness to Him.

Lord, give me strength today to withstand any type of persecution or insult coming my way. Help me to forgive those who have hurt me, those who seem to hate me because of You. Lord I declare that those people will soon know You, that they will know your love and your forgiveness. Lord I pray for those around the world struggling with choosing you over their reputation, also guide them with your strength, confidence, peace, and mercy. Amen.

Day 7:

The blood speaks a better word.

Ephesians 1:7 - "We have redemption in Him through His blood, the forgiveness of our trespasses, according to the riches of His grace."

The blood speaks a better word. Whatever battle, addiction, stress, financial trouble, or heartache you are going through the blood of Jesus speaks a better word. You may have felt like you've had brokenness and despair spoken over you, but that is not your destiny. You have redemption in Him through His blood and because of that all things are under His feet. So, whatever you are facing today, just remember that the blood of Jesus has the final say in the matter. All may look lost around you, but there is no need to stress anymore, because the blood speaks a better word.

God, I thank you for sending your Son Jesus to die for me. I thank you that He rose from the dead. I declare right now over my life that the blood of Jesus speaks a better and final word. No longer does depression or hurt have a hold on me, but in Jesus name I am free. I speak all this in Jesus name. Amen.

Day 8:

If you're too big to do something small, you're too small to do something big.

Colossians 3:23 - "Whatever you do, do it enthusiastically, as something done for the Lord and not for men."

Many people want to stand on a platform, but few are willing to build it. We are called to do whatever God has called us to do with enthusiasm and passion. God will not raise you up until He knows and sees He can trust you with the little things. No act of service or work done for Him is insignificant, but rather it is often doing the 'small things' right that launch us into our big destinies. If you are too prideful to clean bathrooms, take out the trash, help others, or even doing anything not in the spotlight, you will never build the character necessary to sustain the 'big things.'

So today, remember that it is the 'little things' that make way for God to use you for the 'big things'.

Lord, today I ask that you humble me. Help me to see that no job or task is insignificant, but rather when I do it with enthusiasm it honors you. From today onwards I will give my all to whatever it is you place in front of me big or small, spotlight or no spotlight. I never want to take for granted the opportunity to serve you. Amen.

Day 9:

Quit being so tied down.

John 8:36 - "Therefore, if the Son sets you free, you really will be free."

Christ has set you free! You are not obligated to a single person. You are not obligated to Youtube or Netflix, but rather Christ has set you free! Many times certain things in our lives act as lassos and rope us in. Some of you are still tied down, because you feel obligated to keep that person around or binge that new series. You are not obligated to anything besides the Father! Those things are just distractions to keep you from living in the true freedom found in Jesus. You owe it to God to be free and pursue the best you! Jesus came so that you could have life overflowing with freedom and true satisfaction! So today, take some time to identify what has you tied down and see how you can begin to move past that!

Jesus, today I commit my life to you again. I receive your freedom for my life. Help me to realize what is tying me down. Surround me with your peace, courage, and protection to overcome these lassos in my life. I commit myself to live for you. In the name of Jesus I am free. Amen.

Day 10:

When prayer becomes your habit, miracles become your lifestyle.

James 5:16 - "Therefore, confess your sins to one another and pray for one another, so that you may be healed. The urgent request of a righteous person is very powerful in its effect."

We are called to a lifestyle of prayer that cultivates miracles. We are called to a lifestyle of prayer that sees the impossible be ordinary and the super become natural. I love the thought of this and that scripture, because it doesn't say anything about praying 'good enough' or 'huge crazy things', it just says that our prayers as children of God are powerful and effective. The more prayer becomes a habit for you, the more miracles you will see. This is true, because the more time we spend with Him the more we begin to talk, act, and see how He does

. If we want to see the impossible done in our lives, we must first lay the groundwork in the prayer place. Today, commit to a life of prayer and have confidence in Him to come through in miracles.

Lord, I declare for the impossible to happen in and through my life. Use me for miracles, for revival, for salvations, and for financial breakthrough in other peoples lives. Thank you that I can approach you with confidence knowing that you want what is best for me. Help me to always posture myself towards prayer and being with You. Amen.

Day 11:

Death is only part of the process.

John 3:16 "For God loved the world in this way: He gave His One and Only Son, so that everyone who believes in Him will not perish but have eternal life."

Thanatophobia - the fear of death. Death is a disease each human on Earth has and will never get rid of. If we take our eyes off of Jesus it can be so easy to fear death. The pain, sorrow, and devastation it brings has affected us all. But as John 3:16 so brilliantly tells us, God has made a way out. If we call on the name of Jesus and confess that He is Lord then surely we will have eternal life with Him. Death no longer becomes the end, but is now just part of the process. Jesus overcame death and grave so you no longer have to live in fear of death. Know today that death isn't the end, but rather is the means by which you will finally get to see Jesus face to face.

Thank you Jesus for defeating death and hell. You won the victory for me so I no longer have to fear death. Open my eyes to the reality of having enteral life in you and help me to no longer be afraid of death. Thank you for saving my soul. Amen.

Day 12:

Many times God will provide a way through, not a way out.

Romans 15:4-5 - "For everything that was written in the past was written to teach us, so that through the endurance taught in the Scriptures and the encouragement they provide we might have hope. May the God who gives endurance and encouragement give you the same attitude of mind toward each other that Christ Jesus had."

Trials and tribulations are all things we face in life. Whether it's the death of a loved one, a lost relationship, financial hardship, or mental illness we all go through things. We live in a broken world and these things are bound to happen. In the Bible we see the story of the Israelites being enslaved in Egypt. I'm sure they wanted an immediate way out from slavery, but God didn't do that for them.

Instead He sent Moses to negotiate and deal with Pharaoh. Now this wasn't an instant fix to their situation nor did it make things better at first. God's people had to learn what it meant to endure for a period of time. Maybe you are reading this and find yourself in a rut and maybe you even feel like a slave to your situation. While God is always on time, many times He won't take you out right away, but He will always bring you through. His plan for you may be to learn endurance, learn trust, learn patience, and learn faithfulness.

God will guide you step by step and prayer by prayer, but you have to endure. God eventually brought the Israelites through the Red Sea and wanted to lead them to the promised land. When you choose to endure it allows God to create a way through and gives you access to the 'promised land' God has for you. Today, keep enduring with the same mind of Christ, for in due time God will bring you through.

Thank you Lord that all things work together for my good. Even though I feel like I'm stuck in slavery I will endure until I see the promised land. Thank you that your way through is much better than my way out. I ask for the patience, strength, and faith to endure. I know that you will bring me though and until that moment comes I'm leaning on you with all I have. Amen.

Day 13:

God wants to walk with you

Genesis 5:24 - "Enoch walked faithfully with God; then he was no more, because God took him away."

I don't know what kind of God you grew up hearing about, maybe it was an angry God or a distant God. We are constantly fed all these ideas about who He is and how our relationship with Him should be. Can I tell you today that God wants to be your friend. He is not out to get you. He is not angry with you. He is patiently waiting for you to return His calls. He is so eager to spend time with you! I can see God up in heaven just leaning on the edge of His seat in anticipation saying "Are they going to pray today?!", "Do they know I love them?!", "Hey! Hey! Open The Bible, I want to say something that will help you!"

The truth is like a best friend, God cares about each little detail of your day, He cares about your big moments and your shameful moments. God is a God of the mountain tops and a God of the valleys. Just like Enoch, He longs for us to walk with Him in fellowship. So today, take some extra time to be in His presence and just try being His friend.

Father, I come to you today with an open heart and open mind. Thank you that you want to be my friend. Thank you that you don't look at my past as terms and conditions to our relationship.
Thank you for being my friend, someone I can turn to and talk to. You've had my back since you formed me in my mother's womb and I'm so grateful for that. I'm sorry for the times I've kept you waiting on me and even turned my back on you. Today I commit myself to strengthening our relationship forever. Amen.

Day 14:

God's plan for me is one of power and goodness.

Romans 8:28 - "And we know that for those who love God all things work together for good, for those who are called according to his purpose"

God has a good plan for your life. Often times we try to do things our way or alone and it never quite works out. I remember in high school I used to be closed off and never share my thoughts with anyone. Looking back I realized how much it hindered God's plan for my life. I fought so many battles alone and never really had anyone to help me through my valleys. God wants to give you great things and use you mightily, but He cannot do that if you try to do things on your own. God's plan for you is one of power and goodness for your life.

Today, try to relax and rest in the fact that God has your life under HIs control. In the palm of His hand is the best place you could ever be. Stop trying so hard to control your life and allow Him to show you how good He really is!

Thank you God that your plan for my life is filled with your power and goodness. Thank you that I don't have to worry about how things will work out when I know you are on my side. Help me to see your divine hand at work in my everyday life. I commit to being present and persistent in honor you with my time, efforts, and plans. Amen.

Day 15:

God's plan for me is one of peace and shelter.

Psalm 37:1-5 — "Do not fret because of evil men or be envious of those who do wrong for like the grass they will soon wither, like green plants they will soon die away. Trust in the LORD and do good; dwell in the land and enjoy safe pasture. Delight yourself in the LORD and he will give you the desires of your heart. Commit your way to the LORD; trust in him and he will do it."

In a world full of war, famine, poverty, and lack it can be easy to lose trust in God's safety and protection. God's desire is to give you peace and shelter in Him. Scripture tells us to trust in the Lord and do good and we will enjoy "safe pasture." When we align our lives with God's, He will give us supernatural safety and peace. If you commit your way to knowing Him you will know what peace is! God is your source of peace and shelter.

You can trust Him to protect you in the good and bad times. He is our ever present help in time of need. Today, make an effort to intentionally receive His peace and shelter for you.

Lord, thank you that your plan for my life is one of peace and shelter. I thank you that I can turn to you in times of need and you'll surround me with comfort and safety. Continue to guide me throughout my day and week, I release worry and restlessness from my life and I receive your peace and shelter. Amen.

Day 16:

Forgive as easily as you are offended.

Ephesians 4:31-32 - "Get rid of all bitterness, rage and anger, brawling and slander, along with every form of malice. Be kind and compassionate to one another, forgiving each other, just as in Christ God forgave you."

I'm sure every person reading this at one point or another has been offended. While forgiving someone is much easier said than done Jesus never called us to do easy. The thing about hanging on to an offense is it only hurts you. Each day you hold on to this dead baggage is more weight you add on to carry. Maybe the reason you feel so exhausted all the time is because you are carrying around a burden that wasn't meant for you to carry. We are commanded to forgive others as Christ has forgiven us.

In fact, we are supposed to forgive just as easily as we are offended. Think about that for a second. The good news is you have help because Jesus knows what it feels like to have to forgive all of mankind. You are not in this alone! Today, focus on forgiving those around you and letting go of past offenses that are holding you back!

Lord, help me to forgive those who have hurt me. I am tired of carrying around empty baggage. Thank you for forgiving me on that cross. No longer will I let offense be my portion, but rather the forgiveness you won for me will be my response. Amen.

Day 17:

Don't neglect thanking God for the miracle.

1 Thessalonians 5:18 - "Give thanks in all circumstances; for this is God's will for you in Christ Jesus."

Today is a miracle. Your life is a miracle. The fact that you are alive and able to breathe is a miracle. The fact that you have received salvation is a miracle. There are so many things God has done in our lives that we have to be thankful for. Often, we forget to thank God for the miracle He has done in our lives. As a Father, He just wants to hear "thank you" from you! When we begin to thank God for all that He is and all that He has done it opens up doors of blessing, contentment, and value on your life.

You will see things in a new light and experience His presence in a new way! Today, make an effort to write down or list out the miracles God has done in your life! It can be as simple as family and friends or as big as healings and breakthrough, God just wants your heart and gratitude.

Thank you God for the miracles you have done in my life. I'm sorry at times that I have neglected to thank you for your wondrous works. It is your will for my life that I live from a place of thankfulness. Open my eyes to see your goodness and miracles in all seasons. I thank you that your continuous right hand is on my life. Amen.

Day 18:

Can God trust you?

2nd Peter 1:5-8 - "For this very reason, make every effort to add to your faith goodness; and to goodness, knowledge; and to knowledge, self-control; and to self-control, perseverance; and to perseverance, godliness; and to godliness, mutual affection; and to mutual affection, love. For if you possess these qualities in increasing measure, they will keep you from being ineffective and unproductive in your knowledge of our Lord Jesus Christ."

Can God trust you? Can He trust you with finances, character, opportunities, and with blessing? How you handle each daily decision now is determining how much God can trust you with. He is watching to see who He can trust to raise up and lead revival. God isn't about the talent, gifts, or dreams you have. He is about your character.

God has equipped you with everything you need to be successful, but it's on you to earn His trust for the greater things Jesus spoke about. God will not raise you up until you've lived a life behind the scenes that is worthy of the spotlight. When God does put the spotlight on your life it only magnifies everything, so it is vital we build character now. The thing that will sustain you in that spotlight is staying true to who you were before all 'the stuff' happens. God wants to bless you, but can He really trust you? Make an effort today to pursue goodness, knowledge, self-control, perseverance, godliness, mutual affection, and love.!

Father, today I come to you knowing I have things I need to work on. I want your hand of favor on my life, but I know I need to fix some character issues in my life. Help me to see these areas and give me the strength through your Holy Spirit to change these issues. Thank you for the opportunity to partner with you in bringing Heaven to Earth. Amen.

Day 19:

The world may have overlooked you, but God is looking over you.

Jeremiah 1:5 - "Before I formed you in the womb I knew you, before you were born I set you apart; I appointed you as a prophet to the nations."

You may be like me, overlooked your whole life. I grew up living on fire for God, preached my first sermon at 13, started a student led church at age 15, led the church for 7 years, spoke at all the county schools and a few near me, worked on staff at a church, yet my whole life I was overlooked. Rarely and I mean rarely did I ever receive a "good job," "I'm so proud of you," "here's some good advice," my whole life I was overlooked by man. When others who 'didn't deserve it' got opportunities or recognition I had to sit back and keep quiet behind the scenes.

Often times because I was so devout I would even be left out of things by other people. Maybe you are like me, doing the right thing for the right reasons, but it feels like no one cares. Here is the truth: God cares, God is proud of you, and God sees you. Each time you do something for Him, He is shouting from Heaven "well done good and faithful servant." Today, you are not forgotten nor abandoned, but the Creator of the universe is zoomed in on your life smiling. He knew you before you ever knew yourself. He formed you before you could even comprehend you had a heartbeat. The world may have overlooked you, but God is looking over you.

Thank you Lord that you see me. I thank you that I am not forgotten, thank you that you are proud of me. I declare today that your approval is the only thing I need, that regardless of my desire for attention, the affection you have for me is enough. Help me focus on your love for me. Amen.

Day 20:

You have to seek out the anointing of God.

Corinthians 1:21-22 "Now it is God who makes both us and you stand firm in Christ. He anointed us, set his seal of ownership on us, and put his Spirit in our hearts as a deposit, guaranteeing what is to come."

God has anointed you for great things. There is an anointing on your life to live as Jesus did with words of power, miracles, and breakthrough blessing, but it has to be labored for. This kind of anointing takes hours of prayer, living right, and knowing the Word of God. It doesn't matter if you 'have,' 'say,' or 'do' all the right things, if you have not labored for the anointing of God you will not see true growth or lasting fruit. We must learn to go into the secret place and yearn for the anointing that breaks yokes and bondages.

We can not afford to know everything else yet not know His face, not know His love, or not even know His beauty. His face shines with glory that makes man tremble! You have a great anointing placed over your life, but you must labour for it. God will begin to pour it out over your life as you continue to be desperate for Him.

Thank you Lord for your anointing. Thank you that my life is anointed, I ask that you would give me the desire to labour and spend time with you. May I never give up in pursuing the same power and anointing Jesus had that shaped all of humanity forever. I receive your anointing that sealed my life to yours. Amen.

Day 21:

Leaders are willing to walk through valleys so others can stand on mountaintops.

Matthew 20:26 - "Whoever wants to become great among you must be your servant, and whoever wants to be first must be your slave — just as the Son of Man did not come to be served, but to serve, and to give his life as a ransom for many."

Whoever is reading this you are a leader! Whether or not you like it, you are leading someone around you. As leaders people are constantly looking at us for answers and direction. We must be willing to go through valleys so that the people looking to us can experience the mountaintops. This means we must be willing to sacrifice our time, energy, convenience, and habits to the cause of reaching people for Christ. There's a picture that went viral a few years ago of a zoomed in pack of wolves rather easily walking through a very deep snow trail.

The picture then zoomed out to show the leader who is ahead of the pack making a trail for them to follow. This wolf not only made an easier path for them to follow through its hard work, but also ran the risk of being attacked by predators lurking in the snow . What an amazing image of what it means to lead others. God has called us to make a clear path to Jesus for those around us and to be willing and vulnerable at all times in order to make sure we lead our pack closer to Jesus. Today, realize that God has placed you in a position of leadership and know that it comes with a worthy cost. Be encouraged that you get to participate in what He is doing on the Earth, you get to impact eternity and nothing compares to that.

Lord, give me the strength today to walk through the valleys of leaderships. Fix my eyes on the mountain top others will experience when I'm going through a valley. Encourage every leader blazing trails for their people to walk through. Thank you for calling me to lead others. Amen.

Day 22:

It's your move.

Hebrews 1:15-18 - "The Son is the image of the invisible God, the firstborn over all creation. For in Him all things were created, things in heaven and on earth, visible and invisible, whether thrones or dominions or rulers or authorities. All things were created through Him and for Him. He is before all things, and in Him all things hold together. And He is the head of the body, the church; He is the beginning and firstborn from among the dead, so that in all things He may have preeminence."

I wonder if sometimes God gets annoyed at us asking Him to "do it again." Heal again, come again, and send revival again. As if He needs so much persuading to move and love the Earth. We are not waiting on Him to move, He is waiting on us to move. Jesus said we would do even greater things than He did. He has sent us one named the Holy Spirit who is greater than Him.

You have both the resurrection power and the Holy Spirit living in you! You carry healing, revival, peace, hope, joy, and the life and love of Jesus. You have the answer a broken world is looking for! Don't allow yourself to only pray and not activate your faith for God to overflow on the Earth through you! Be brave. You carry the answer. Today, remember that in Him are all things and for Him all are things. All that we need to change the world is at our disposal, it's our move.

Lord, I declare in the name of Jesus that I will see an increase of miracles, salvations, healings, and signs and wonders for your glory. I thank you that emotional, physical, mental, and spiritual health are my portion. I thank you that you are moving even now as I pray. I believe you are stirring something in my that will shape my school, university, workplace, and the nations of the Earth. Thank you for bringing Heaven to Earth just because I asked. Amen.

Day 23:

Often times the person you want to love the least is the person who needs it the most.

Galatians 6:9 - "Let us not become weary in doing good, for at the proper time we will reap a harvest if we do not give up."

Let's be honest, people are tough. Especially those who make it so stinking hard to love them. I remember a couple years ago I had someone close to me go through a rough patch in life. This person hurt me, put me in terrible situations, and said unspeakable things to me. Now I had a choice to either be bitter and let it bring me down or I could choose to not give up doing good and love them. God calls us to love people others even when they are at their worst not just when you benefit from loving them. God never gives up on us, so we can never give up on others. Who in your life are you giving up on?

The people who seem to test us the most are often times secretly searching for the answer we have. I can tell you now, because I never stopped loving and praying for this person they are now back on the right track towards God! So today, don't give up loving, for in due time you will reap a harvest in Jesus name!

Lord, give me patience to love those who make life difficult. Help me to see them through your eyes. Help me to learn how to forgive and move on. You created me to love others as you love me. I declare turn around for the struggling in the name of Jesus and that which once was a sore spot in this relationship will become a launchpad for their destiny. Amen.

Day 24:

God doesn't owe you anything.

Psalms 24:1-2 "The earth is the LORD's, and everything in it, the world, and all who live in it; for he founded it on the seas and established it on the waters"

We need to be careful to not get tricked into thinking God "owes" us something. It can be easy to think because we gave an offering that God owes us a bunch of finances and that soon we will be rich or because we prayed with someone today surely God owes us "greater" opportunities. Yes, God will provide and open doors for you, but that kind of thinking can lead to an entitlement relationship. That is dangerous because it also leads to a reward or merit based relationship with God which is also poisonous for your relationship with Him.

We are called to give, love and serve others so they can see, hear, and know the gospel of Jesus. In return we know we are seen, heard, and loved by God and that is more rewarding than any earthly thing we could ever get from Him. So today, remember to be content with where you are and know that God doesn't owe you anything, but rather freely gives.

Thank you Lord that you are My Provider. I trust that you have me right where you want me. Help me not to feel entitled or as if you owe me things for serving you. Give me a humble heart that seeks only you. Amen.

Day 25:

Today's thought: You are God's masterpiece.

Ephesians 2:10 - "For we are God's masterpiece. He has created us anew in Christ Jesus, so we can do the good things he planned for us long ago."

An artist's greatest accomplishment is their own finished work. God's most proud work of art is you! From the beginning of time you were planned and created for His glory! Because you are God's masterpiece, He has great things planned for your life! You are not a mistake, but you do have a purpose! Your identity comes from who He says you are and the rest of the worlds noise is pointless to listen to. The devil may call you names and try to hang things over your heard, but the only paint that can dry on your canvas is the one from the pastor Creator.

His words about you are the most powerful picture ever painted. As you go throughout your day today remind yourself that you are a masterpiece. Hold your head up high and confident as a son or daughter of the universe's master artist.

Lord thank you for creating me. I do not take for granted this life you have woven together. I am your masterpiece, you're most prized possession. Open my eyes to that reality, thank you again for giving me new life and planning good things for me. I choose today to believe that I am who you say I am. Amen.

Day 26:

Give Him space to be a good Father.

2nd Corinthians 1:3-4 - "Blessed be the God and Father of our Lord Jesus Christ, the Father of mercies and God of all comfort, who comforts us in all our affliction, so that we may be able to comfort those who are in any affliction, with the comfort with which we ourselves are comforted by God."

Can God just "be Himself" around you or is He constantly quieted by request, by complaint, by anger, or by need. Imagine with me you are dying to see a loved one, but when you finally see them all they do is complain, ask for money, and ask for things they want. That's not a good way to build a healthy relationship! Yes, God is there for your needs and hurts, but we were created to "just be" with God.

He longs for us to spend time with Him. This is our purpose at its core; to be in fellowship with Him. So today, ask yourself, is my time with God allowing Him to speak to me? As a child are you giving Him space to be a good Father? He already knows what you need, so just be.

Father, thank you that your heart burns for me. I commit to making space in our relationship to "just be" with you. You know my needs, so help me to just allow you to be a good Father during our time together. I ask that your presence would just surround me as I go throughout my day today. Amen.

Day 27:

People can be contagious without ever showing symptoms.

Proverbs 18:24 - "One who has unreliable friends soon comes to ruin, but there is a friend who sticks closer than a brother."

Who is in your circle? The people closest to you always influence you the most. I remember getting close to a friend of mine here at college and adopting some of his speech, thoughts, and even his laugh (weird I know), but also I had another friend say how weird it was, because this same friend was now like a mini version of me. Whether or not we know it the people closest to us influence our actions the most. Don't get tricked into allowing just anyone to speak into your life, as the enemy looks to distract you from your destiny with relationships.

The person you admire or are in a close relationship with may end up being toxic. You must be careful with how you allow them to speak into your life. Remember today, that each relationship you allow into your life is leading you down some path.

Thank you Lord that you have good and healthy relationships out there for me. You designed us to live in community with one another and I value that. I receive the wisdom to discern who should be speaking into my life and who I need to let go of. Thank you for the divine relationships coming my way. Amen.

Day 28:

Nail it to the tree.

Colossians 2:14 - "He erased the certificate of debt, with its obligations, that was against us and opposed to us, and has taken it out of the way by nailing it to the cross."

We all have a past and we all have a future. There is no reason that the latter should affect the later. Jesus has erased our certificate of debt meaning who you were before Him has been washed clean. We carry guilt and shame around like it has us in a prison cell. Jesus nailed your past to the cross way before you were ever even born. Think about this, before your battle, your pain, your hurts, Jesus already took care of it. Quit paying for something Jesus already covered the bill on. The devil doesn't deserve one piece of your life.

The devil works as a debt collector just trying to rack up guilt and shame on you. It is time you nail it to the tree and move on in Jesus name! Today, know that Jesus has already overcome your past by dying and rising again! You have a future full of joy and life now! Make the choice to nail it to the tree called Calvary.

Lord, today I give you my past. I give you everything and everyone that has ever hurt me or caused me to stumble. Today I nail whatever has been hindering me to the tree of Calvary and just as you did I declare "It is finished" in the name of Jesus. Thank you for freedom and forgiveness. Amen.

Day 29:

He is worthy of worship despite how you feel.

1 Samuel 15:22 - "But Samuel replied: 'Does the LORD delight in burnt offerings and sacrifices as much as in obeying the LORD? To obey is better than sacrifice, and to heed is better than the fat of rams."

As Christians we can place this expectation on ourselves that we are always supposed to feel good worshiping or be the most on fire all the time for every service, but that couldn't be further from the truth. There will be times where you won't want to worship and moments you won't always see the point of worshipping. True worship comes when you decide in that moment that despite what you feel He is still worthy of praise over and over again. In that moment of obedience heaven and earth collide and our hearts align with His.

It is vital we understand this, because worship was never about us in the first place. Worship has never been about what we get from it, but always about what can we give back to God. So today, know that it's okay to feel like you don't want to worship, but also realize that God is so worthy of every single second of your life. True worship is when we obey the call to honor Him no matter how we feel.

Lord, today I make the choice to worship you. I will not listen to how I feel or the circumstances around me. You are so holy and worthy to be praised. Let your presence and discipline flood my life. Your hand at play around me is evident in everything I do. Thank you for being a God so worthy of worship, so worthy of honoring when how I feel goes out the window. I give you my best, because you are worthy of it. Amen.

Day 30:

When God speaks, listen.

Psalm 18:30 - "As for God, his way is perfect: The Lord's word is flawless; He shields all who take refuge in him."

There is power in each word God speaks. Every syllable off of His tongue is profound. Just a whisper from Him shifts situations, breaks addictions, and empties the grave! Mountains move even at the quiver of His lips. God's way is perfect. Don't make the mistake of dismissing when you hear from God or not obeying what He speaks to you! If you let Him, just a single word off of His lips can change your life. When God speaks there is no taking Him lightly, because all authority in the universe is in each word He speaks. So today, take the time to listen to His voice and obey.

Lord, open my ears to hear you more clearly. Change my perspective to understand just how powerful and amazing each word you speak is. Your words have the power to change my life and I am so grateful for that. Thank you that your way is perfect. Thank you that you are my refuge and shield. Amen.

Day 31:

God has always been there.

Genesis 28:15 - "I am with you and will watch over you wherever you go, and I will bring you back to this land. I will not leave you until I have done what I have promised you."

I remember when was in my mid-teens and going through a rough season in my walk with God. I was choosing sin and feeding my bad habits rather than obeying Him. This led to me feeling so empty inside. I remember one time I messed up bad and I was angry at myself so I went into the bathroom and locked the door. I stared at the mirror and couldn't even recognize who I had become. I remember feeling so numb even wondering if I was human. I stood there face to face with the worst of me and just wept.

A few years after the Lord showed me a vision where He took me back to that moment (like the Ghost of Christmas past), but He showed me that moment in the mirror. He showed me His Spirit standing behind me and in that moment He was also in pain, also crying out on my behalf. He then said to me "I was there the whole time." When I felt my worst and most alone God was still there. Someone reading this needs to know that God has been with you the whole time. God has not abandoned you and He never will. When you hurt He hurts, when you cry He cries, when you battle He battles on your behalf. His word says He will not leave you until He does what He promised. God has promised you freedom, joy, and peace. He will not quit until these things come to pass. So today, remember that God is on your side and He always has been!

Lord, come surround me today. I surrender my pain to you. I receive your promise of freedom and joy. Holy Spirit reawaken my heart to burn for you.

Day 32:

Jesus the stone roller, not the stone thrower.

John 8:6-8 - "Jesus bent down and wrote with his finger in the dirt. They kept at him, badgering him. He straightened up and said, "The sinless one among you, go first: throw the stone."

Jesus came down from Heaven to Earth to cleanse us from our sins. At His first coming He did not come to judge, but to forgive and display the Father's love for us. In the story mentioned in today's scripture we pick up where the Pharisees are about to stone a lady for cheating on her husband, but instead Jesus (who is perfect and had every right to) joining in with them, He puts a stop to it.

Fast forward to the resurrection scene and Scripture tells us that the stone covering His tomb has been rolled away for He has risen. Here's why we have cause to celebrate, because regardless of our sin Jesus came to roll our stones away rather than throw them at us. He came to set us free from the curse of death. Jesus had every right to condemn us, but instead He picks us up and gives us our own resurrection. Today, take a second to reflect on the grace and mercy of Jesus who rolled away the stone of death once and for all.

Thank you Jesus for your sacrifice. Thank you that you didn't come to condemn us, but rather to make a way for us to have eternal life. Thank you that you aren't a stone thrower, but a stone roller. I receive your resurrection power for my life. Amen.

Day 33:

Your attitude and work ethic can either rob you or release you into God's supernatural blessing.

Galatians 6:7 - "Do not be deceived: God cannot be mocked. A man reaps what he sows."

I've never been one to work on a farm, but I do know that in order to reap a harvest you first have to plow, plant, grow, and then you can finally harvest. Success and blessing from God do not come overnight. You must first plow (that means hard work), then you must plant (that means sacrificing and investing in what He has called you to), then you have to grow (put in the effort to grow as a person/at your craft), and finally you can harvest (supernatural blessing of God). God has a principle: you reap what you sow.

Many times we miss out on His blessing, because we are too busy complaining about our current situation or making excuses for our life. God blesses hard, authentic, and sacrificial work! You have greatness in you, don't ruin it by complaining! Today, make an effort to do what you can do and God will take care of the rest!

Lord, help me to have a good work ethic and attitude. I surrender my complaining to you and I know that you will bless the work of my hand. I thank you for your divine favor and blessing coming my way. Amen.

Day 34:

Turn your eyes upon Jesus.

Hebrews 12:1-2 - "Therefore, since we are surrounded by such a great cloud of witnesses, let us throw off everything that hinders and the sin that so easily entangles. And let us run with perseverance the race marked out for us, fixing our eyes on Jesus, the pioneer and perfecter of faith. For the joy set before him he endured the cross, scorning its shame, and sat down at the right hand of the throne of God."

We live in a world full of constant distractions. We live to be entertained and occupied. It seems as if each and every thing at every moment is trying to grab our attention. The enemy will do everything in his power to distract you. He knows if he can keep you from knowing The Bible and from encountering God's presence then he wins. What you focus on is the reality you create. I want to encourage you to fix your eyes upon Jesus.

Do not get caught up in the glamour of this world, but realize that He is the end goal and the ultimate prize. He is the lover of your soul and He desires to bring you into close relationship with Him, but distractions so often get in the way. He did not endure the cross to become a side dish! He is the appetizer, side dish, main meal, dessert, and living water for your soul. He is everything! Jesus endured the cross so He could have a close and intimate relationship with you. Today, take time to look at your life and see what is distracting you from being close to Him.

Jesus help me to see the distractions in my life. I'm sorry for allowing things get in the way of our relationship. Help me to see the things that need to go, I want to draw near to you. So today I fix my eyes on you and you alone. Amen.

Day 35:

Sometimes you have to dance your way out.

2nd Samuel 6:14-15 - "And David danced before the Lord with all his might, wearing a priestly garment. So David and all the people of Israel brought up the Ark of the Lord with shouts of joy and the blowing of rams' horns."

I would like to think I know how to dance well, but reality is those who know me would definitely have a second opinion. In my time with the Lord I have found that dancing before Him and in His presence is one of the most powerful and transformative things you could do. There is so much joy and power in dancing before Him. For me, it usually is just jumping up and down when I'm fired up in His presence or in prayer. Other times it looks like actual dancing, but there is something so liberating and powerful about dancing in His presence.

If you are going through a difficult time, get in His presence and dance it out. Scripture says that David danced before the Lord with all his might and that those around him experienced deep joy because his dancing! The joy of the Lord is your strength! Dancing before Him is just an outward expression of an inward encounter with Him! Sometimes you have to dance your way out.

Lord, fill me with your joy so much that my only reaction is to dance before you. I ask that you would give me the courage to worship in a new way and that as I begin to be filled with your joy chains would break off on my life. I thank you that my worship doesn't only impact me, but touches those around me. I'm believing to encounter you like I never have before. Amen.

Day 36:

Step out of the boat!

Matthew 14:27-30 - "But Jesus immediately said to them: "Take courage! It is I. Don't be afraid." "Lord, if it's you," Peter replied, "tell me to come to you on the water." "Come," he said. Then Peter got down out of the boat, walked on the water and came toward Jesus."

I think it is safe to say we all want to see the impossible done in our lives right? I think it is also safe to say that not a lot of us want to step out of the boat that leads to the impossible. Staying in the boat is safe, it's comfortable, and it can be sustained by self-reliance. Here's the thing: Jesus has called us to a life of the impossible, a life of walking on water with Him. His call to the impossible is not safe, it is not comfortable, and it requires you depend on Him 1,000,000% of the time.

Here's the tough news: People will never get saved as long as you stay in the boat. It is time that some of you reading this take a step faith out onto the water, because that's where Jesus is inviting you. So today, know that you can step out of the boat and do the impossible alongside Jesus. He has called you to great and marvelous things, but it starts with stepping out of the boat.

Jesus, thank you that you've called me to a life of the impossible. Help me not to rely on myself or my own safety net anymore, but to solely depend on your power and faithfulness that sustains me. I thank you that when I step out of the boat salvations for will follow. Amen.

Day 37:

Take the time to listen to others.

Romans 12:3 - "Because of the privilege and authority God has given me, I give each of you this warning: Don't think you are better than you really are. Be honest in your evaluation of yourselves, measuring yourselves by the faith God has given us."

One of the most valuable skills you can have in today's society is the ability to listen. So often it can be about what I have to say or what am I going to say next instead of genuinely trying to listen and understand someone. We have become numb to the idea of hearing others out and seek only to get our point across or be recognized for how we think. Jesus was a great listener. He stopped several times to listen to peoples needs and just be there for them. I think one of the most powerful actions of love you can show in todays world is being there for someone.

It is so rare to find someone who genuinely cares about what you have to say. Today, be that person for someone. Many people come from messed up homes or backgrounds where no one has ever cared about what they have to say. You do not have to agree with someone to value what they are saying and who they are. Reach out and grab a coffee with someone who needs to be heard. It will leave you with the best feeling ever, I promise.

Lord, I'm sorry for being selfish and only thinking of myself in a conversation. Help me to place value on what others are saying and thinking. Show me opportunities around me to value others as you value each one of us. Amen.

Day 38:

Jesus is always fully Himself.

Hebrews 1:3 - "The Son is the radiance of God's glory and the exact representation of his being, sustaining all things by his powerful word. After he had provided purification for sins, he sat down at the right hand of the Majesty in heaven."

In the landscape of todays culture it can be so easy to have doubts about your faith in Jesus. So many people are trying to tell you what to believe and how to believe it. If you are having doubts about your faith in Jesus; I've come to encourage that Jesus is always fully Himself. He is always the healer, always a lover, always a friend, always there, always resurrecting, always constant, always the highest power, and always seated at the right hand of God.

It is impossible for Jesus to ever change, because since the beginning of time He has always fully been Himself. So today, be reassured that Jesus is who He says He is and will do what He said He will do in your life.

Jesus, thank you that you are always fully yourself. You never hide any pieces of who you are away for me, but invite me to discover the majesty of who you are. Thank you that from today forward I will no longer doubt who you are, but I step into the confidence of knowing you and your finished work. Amen.

Day 39:

Don't settle for just a 'sip' of Jesus.

Psalm 34:8 - "Taste and see that the Lord is good; blessed is the one who takes refuge in him."

Imagine, you have the entire worlds supply of pizza at your hands I mean enough to last you for forever, but because you have the wrong mentality you don't enjoy it. Instead of eating to your stomachs contentment you take just a little bite and leave the table. We tend to do this with God, He has given us all we need in Him, yet we just take a little bite and leave the table. Even though at this table is the fullness of satisfaction, healing, rest, blessing, and purpose we settle for a bite and miss out on a feast. God spread the table thin when He sent Jesus to die for our sins and yet we only want a small bite of Him.

We are okay with a Sunday service or just the daily you-version reminder and while these things are great we are living off of a 'sip' mentality. God has so much more for you than you could ever imagine! You just need to realize that He has already prepared everything you need! So today, make an extra effort to be in His presence and really dig deep to pursue Him in all things and watch how your life changes!

Lord, I don't want just enough of you. I need all of you in my daily life. I admit I can not do this alone, but I need the fullness of who you are to come into my life. I open up my heart to receive you completely. Thank you for being good to me at all times. Amen.

Day 40:

God gives us rules not to limit us, but to protect us.

Psalm 119: 97-101 - "Oh, how I love Your law! It is my meditation all the day. You, through Your commandments, make me wiser than my enemies; For they are ever with me. I have more understanding than all my teachers, For Your testimonies are my meditation. I understand more than the ancients, Because I keep Your precepts. I have restrained my feet from every evil way, That I may keep Your word."

I remember there were times early in my faith where I would be mad at God or ask Him why we have to have all these laws and commands . It almost felt like He was the fun police and just wanted me to be bored and miserable all the time. If we aren't careful it can be easy to think God is just some big mean boss ready to zap us if we don't obey everything He says.

This couldn't be further from the truth, God has given us the law to protect us and even to show us how much we truly need Him. The commands are meant to steer us away from the entanglement of sin that so easily traps us. God loves us so much that He has given us a roadmap on how to avoid sin traps that lead to eternal separation. Today, look at the law as a the key to true freedom and not as the pair of handcuffs that put you in prison.

Lord, thank you for the law that guides us. Help me to hide it in my heart and treasure it more than silver or gold. I commit to making it my lifestyle so I can live a holy and pleasing life for you. Amen.

Day 41:

Be willing to talk about the tough things.

Isaiah 5:20 - "Woe to those who call evil good and good evil, who put darkness for light and light for darkness, who put bitter for sweet and sweet for bitter."

We live in a society today that calls good evil and evil good. Sadly, we have begun to compromise what the word of God says with what the world says will make us happy. As Christians it is so vital that we have the courage to talk about the tough things. We can no longer make excuses for sin to have its way. This generation needs Christians who will stand up for the word of God that are full of love and boldness. The world will never accept Jesus if they don't see it modeled before them! Talking about the though things isn't an excuse to be judgmental, but rather an opportunity to display to others that Jesus is the only way to salvation.

So today, be willing to step out and talk about the tough things! Be of good courage for God has gone before you to prepare the way!

Lord, thank you for giving me the truth. Help me not to call evil good and good evil. I receive the courage to have the tough conversations and stand up for your word even when I am the only one. Use me today as I step out to have the tough talks. Amen.

Day 42:

What is on your lips?

Proverbs 18:21 - "The tongue has the power of life and death, and those who love it will eat its fruit."

I'm going to hit you with a question: What are you speaking? Are you speaking life or death? Are you speaking health or sickness? Are you speaking peace or stress? God has given us the power through the authority that is in the name of Jesus to speak life into our situations. We do not realize the true power of our words. God has called you to be a life speaker, not a death speaker! This applies both to you and to those around you! Are you speaking life over others? It is commonly said that "as a man thinketh, so he is," but I raise you one and say "as a man speaketh, so is his reality."

There have been many times in my life where I have spoken God's word over a situation and He came through. We create the reality of what we experience with the words we use and believe. So today, focus on speaking life over yourself, others, and your current situations. God will begin to move in you and through you!

Lord, thank you for giving me the authority to speak life. I realize that my words are either building up things or tearing them down. Give me the wisdom to speak life and only life. Amen.

Day 43:

Let the roots dig deep.

James 5:7-8 - "Therefore be patient, brethren, until the coming of the Lord The farmer waits for the precious produce of the soil, being patient about it, until it gets the early and late rains. You too be patient; strengthen your hearts, for the coming of the Lord is near."

Let me start off today by saying I would like to applaud all of who have recently taken a risk for Jesus. Whether you started a new small group, talked to someone about Jesus, started serving, or let go of something that was holding you back you took a risk. Here's what I know is true: right after you take a risk for Jesus the enemy will do anything in his power to discourage you! You just became a highly valued asset. The enemy will lie and tell you that what God is using you to plant or grow is actual the harvest. Good things take time to develop.

True change and building something that lasts takes time. In fact, if it is taking a long time to build or develop and you are doing it right, then that's a sign of sure sustainability. Don't get discouraged, because you are on the cusp of something great! Keep building, growing, and believing. We like to see success based off just the physical results, but in reality true success is about depth of the roots you plant. So today, be encouraged that your risk isn't in vain, but in fact God is bringing increase to your life!

Lord, I come to you today to say thank you for allowing things to take time. It is so hard to wait sometimes, but help me to see past the lies of the enemy. I know that you are using me for great and mighty things. I declare all of this in your name Jesus. Amen.

Day 44:

Try to spend less time behind a screen and more time in front of someone

Proverbs 27:17 - "Iron sharpens iron, and one man sharpens another."

How much time do you spend in front of a screen on a daily basis? This is an important question, because we are constantly surrounded by a 'fake reality'. That's right, I said a fake reality. People are the why behind what our lives are for yet we spend most of our time preoccupied by our own need for entertainment. Recently, I've found the joy and true life giving power that comes from sitting down with someone face to face and hearing them share their heart.

This is genuinely one of the most amazing feelings on Earth; to just sit down with someone and truly understand who they are. God has called us to sharpen one another through interaction, but we can't become sharp if we don't ever become intentional about investing in others. So today, make an effort to spend less time behind a screen and more time investing in those around you.

Lord, help me to see the value of reaching those around me. Open my eyes to the beauty of seeing others expression of you. Help me to keep my priorities in the right place. Thank you that you designed us to be in fellowship with one another. Today, I commit to investing in and taking the time to sharpen those around me. Amen.

Day 45:

WASH THE DISHES!

Acts 3:19 - "Repent, then, and turn to God, so that he will forgive your sins"

 Imagine with me you are coming home after a long day at school or work and you walk in feeling refreshed to be home only to see a pile of dirty dishes. Now this pile isn't huge yet, but it still is kind of gross to look at. A few days go by and as you eat and fail to wash the dishes because you 'got busy' or were 'too tired' they begin to pile up. As more time passes bacteria and mold began to grow causing a visible change in the condition of your kitchen. Here's the premise: if you don't regularly wash out the dishes they begin to affect the environment they are in. We do the same thing with our spiritual lives. We start to build up and collect sin into our lives.

We allow it to pile on while making excuses about church, prayer, and how Jesus already covered it so you're good. After a while unrepented sin begins to cause visible change in your life for the worse. It is like driving, you constantly have to be realigning the wheel so you don't crash. Repenting causes us to realign our thoughts, hearts, and actions with what He says. Trust me, I'm not saying you have to keep track of every little sin you commit, but it is vital that when you catch yourself living in sin or feel convicted you take a moment to ask for forgiveness. Just like cleaning out the dishes, repentance creates a clean and healthy internal environment. So throughout your day today actively practice asking God for His forgiveness.

God, I repent of my sins today. I ask for your forgiveness and mercy to come wash me clean. I thank you that the blood of Jesus has covered all my sins and because I believe in Him I am truly forgiven. Thank you for the cross and resurrection. Amen.

Day 46:

You are called to shape history.

Matthew 5:16 - "In the same way, let your light shine before men, so that they may see your good works and give glory to your Father in heaven."

God has called you to be a pioneer. A pioneer is someone who is among the first to explore or settle a new country or area. God calls us to pioneer things into existence for His Kingdom. You have the potential in you to shape history. As a christian you are called to "let your light shine before men" so that they "might see your good works and give glory to God." By you stepping out and taking a risk you can change someone's eternity. So go out today and be fearless, be a pioneer, and make a difference for the cause of Christ. It is what you were made for.

Lord, today I give you my life, I surrender all my fears, doubts, and insecurities. I want to make a difference in people's lives, so I ask that you open my eyes to the opportunities all around me. I receive your boldness today and I know I am called to shape history. Thank you for using me. Amen.

Day 47:

The goal of your life is not to be made famous, but to have intimacy with God.

Psalm 73:28 - "But as for me, the nearness of God is my good; I have made the Lord GOD my refuge, That I may tell of all Your works."

There is so much pressure in our world today to be 'an influencer'. We are encouraged to gain this massive following and then we can be successful. This isn't inherently bad, but can often lead to us being the center of attention and not Jesus. This is why we have churches and leaders who have started selling their name and brand instead of selling the gospel. Again, while leveraging influence in whatever ways possible is necessary to do in today's society, our main focus as believers shouldn't be about how much attention we can get for knowing Him, but rather our lives should be about pouring out our attention at His feet.

We were created for intimacy with God. We were made to know Him and love Him. He sent Jesus to die for us and restore the connection between us and Him. When you begin to have true intimacy with God in due time He will raise you up and give you influence. When He raises you up you'll know that is wasn't anything you ever did, because it will be much more influential and powerful than anything you could have ever accomplished alone. So today, focus on getting to know God better and really being with Him free of motives.

Lord, help me to focus on what really matters and that's being with you. I commit my life not to amassing a bunch of followers, but to truly knowing you. Thank you that you draw near when I call on you. You are my every good thing. Amen.

Day 48:

You can take a deep breath.

Matthew 11:28-30 - "Come to me, all you who are weary and burdened, and I will give you rest. Take my yoke upon you and learn from me, for I am gentle and humble in heart, and you will find rest for your souls. For my yoke is easy and my burden is light."

Today, we are busier than any generation in mankind has ever been. We have millions of workaholics and millions of people consumed by sports and activity day by day. With all the chaos going on around us it makes it nearly impossible to find true rest. Your soul needs rest. Read that sentence again, your soul needs rest. We have become so good at finding distractions which we supplement for rest. It is so crucial you learn what gives your soul true rest!

This is key to your spiritual development and growth. For me, exercise gives me rest (ironic I know), discovering new types of music gives me rest, praying and being in God's presence gives me rest, reflecting gives me rest, and watching the sunset gives me rest. There are many things God has placed around you that can bring your soul rest in Him! So today, take some extra time to rest in Him and find out what replenishes your soul.

Lord, today I take the time to slow down and rest. I receive your supernatural rest and renewing that comes from knowing you and your presence. Help me to find true rest, not just distractions from the business of life. Thank you that you created in me a desire to recharge. I commit to finding the things you've placed around me that bring me joy. Amen.

Day 49:

Discomfort is a call to the next level.

Hebrews 6:1 - "Therefore let us move beyond the elementary teachings about Christ and be taken forward to maturity, not laying again the foundation of repentance from acts that lead to death, and of faith in God."

Wow! Day 49, you are almost half way done! If you're reading this and you've already hit your growth spurt you have definitely experienced something called growing pains! We experience growing pains when our muscles and bones start to develop at a much higher rate than what our bodies are used to you. Today, if you're going through some stretching or pain in your walk with God know that it's just a sign of some growing pains taking place. God may be asking you to give something up or even convicting you about certain habits in your life.

This is a call to the next level of greatness in Him! You were never created to stay at the same level of faith, but as you mature in your walk with God He calls you to a higher level of living! If you are experiencing growing pains, don't worry, because it's a sign you are on the right track!

Lord, thank you for growth. I look back on who I was and realize that you have brought me so far. I ask that you would continue to stretch me as I enter into a new level of relationship with you. Amen.

Day 50:

If you are living for Him you are setting the
standard.

*Psalm 139:14 - "I praise you, for I am fearfully and
wonderfully made. Wonderful are your works; my soul
knows it very well."*

Don't shy away from who you are in God. He
created you to be you. In order for you operate fully
in the gifting He has given you, you have to learn
how to be yourself. God has given you a unique
personality and gift that can reach people others
can't! The devil will convince you that you need to
tone things down, or bring things up, or change
your personality to fit some mold. The only voice
you need to listen to is God's. I promise if you are
being who He has created you to be there's no need
to live up to a certain standard. If you are living for
Him you are the standard.

People are watching what your life looks like and when they see how confident you are in yourself they will want what you have and that is Jesus! So today, take a moment and list out some great qualities you have. Set the standard and watch others follow!

Lord, help me today to be myself. You have created me with unique gifting and a unique personality. I declare that I am not who people say I am or want me to be, but I am who you say I am which is enough. Thank you for allowing me to set the standard by living for you. Amen.

Day 51:

What God can do through you is often dependent on what you first allow Him to do in you.

Romans 12:1-2 - "So here's what I want you to do, God helping you: Take your everyday, ordinary life – your sleeping, eating, going-to-work, and walking-around life – and place it before God as an offering. Embracing what God does for you is the best thing you can do for him. Don't become so well-adjusted to your culture that you fit into it without even thinking. Instead, fix your attention on God. You'll be changed from the inside out. Readily recognize what he wants from you, and quickly respond to it. Unlike the culture around you, always dragging you down to its level of immaturity, God brings the best out of you, develops well-formed maturity in you."

What is your current heart posture towards God? Do you have a closed off posture or an arms open surrendered posture?

Good heart posture is key to receiving all God wants to do in you. Here's the interesting thing about posture, it's all on you. Your heart posture is 100% dependent on what choice you make. If you are sitting hunched over you have the authority to sit up and choose to control your posture. Because of Jesus we can now position our hearts into a close relationship with the Father. He asks us to take our everyday life and just live it surrendered to Him and what He wants to do through you. So today, focus on surrendering your heart to His voice.

Lord, I surrender my life to you. Over and over again my answer is just one big yes to you. Give me the will and discipline to position myself closer to your voice. I look forward to hearing from you today.

Day 52:

Worship is never about the return.

1 Chronicles 16:23-31 - "Sing to the LORD, all the earth; proclaim his salvation day after day. Declare his glory among the nations, his marvelous deeds among all peoples. For great is the LORD and most worthy of praise; he is to be feared above all gods. For all the gods of the nations are idols, but the LORD made the heavens. Splendor and majesty are before him; strength and joy are in his dwelling place. Ascribe to the LORD, all you families of nations, ascribe to the LORD glory and strength. Ascribe to the LORD the glory due his name; bring an offering and come before him. Worship the LORD in the splendor of his holiness. Tremble before him, all the earth! The world is firmly established; it cannot be moved. Let the heavens rejoice, let the earth be glad; let them say among the nations, "The LORD reigns!"

When we worship , God comes in return, but worship is never about the return. Worship is always about emptying ourselves out at His feet. Worship is about who He is, focusing on His splendor, His majesty, His goodness, and His beauty. Often times we worship because we want to feel God; we worship because we want to feel good; we worship because we want to feel better, but in truth worship is never about what we get out of it. Worship is always about giving back to Him what He deserves every moment of every day. His presence is a byproduct, not the focus of worship. If God never gave us His presence , just because of who He is; He would still be worthy of our life song. So today, make time to worship God and focus on who He is!

Lord, you are holy. There is no one like you and there will never be anyone like you. Who can match your greatness? You are high and above everything. You are Creator and Father. You are worthy of my everything. Amen.

Day 53:

God is your cornerman.

Zephaniah 3:15-17 - "The Lord has taken away your punishment, he has turned back your enemy. The Lord, the King of Israel, is with you; never again will you fear any harm. On that day they will say to Jerusalem, "Do not fear, Zion; do not let your hands hang limp. The Lord your God is with you, the Mighty Warrior who saves. He will take great delight in you; in his love he will no longer rebuke you, but will rejoice over you with singing."

In boxing the coach of the boxer is called the cornerman. The cornerman's job is to prepare his fighter for battle, believe in him, and defend him. Just like a cornerman God has equipped you for battle by giving you His word, access to His presence, Jesus, and community with believers. Know today that God believes in you!

You may be in the fight of your life, but He believes in the broken and beaten up you just as much as the victorious and confident you. God also defends you. In boxing sometimes the victor will turn his back to celebrate and the loser will try to get a cheap shot in, but the first one in the ring to defend his fighter is the cornerman. Maybe you are reading this and you feel like you've been cheap shotted by the enemy, but God has sent me to tell you that He's stepping in to defend you! So today, know that God is in your corner!

Lord, thank you for being my cornerman. I thank you that you equip me to fight, that you believe in me, and that you step in on my behalf. Remind me that you are always there for me in the battle of life. Amen.

Day 54:

Worry is often a result of two things: mindset and perspective.

2nd Timothy 1:7 - "For the Spirit God gave us does not make us timid, but gives us power, love and self-discipline."

Worry seems to be one of the biggest problems in today's world. The bible tells us not to worry or be anxious about anything. God has placed in you a spirit of power, love, and discipline so you wouldn't have to be burdened by worry. Worry will try to keep you from moving forward in Him, which is why it is essential you know that the power to overcome is already in you! Today, know that you are an overcomer of worry and that it is not your destiny! God has your life and your needs under control. Trust Him and He will work it out! You can cast your cares upon Him.

Lord, help me to overcome my worry. Life looks a little unclear right now, but I trust you to make a way. I know the power to overcome is in me, so in the name of Jesus I speak peace and wellness over my life. I believe all this will come to pass in Your name. Amen.

Day 55:

You are always one click away from a mistake you can never take back.

Proverbs 4:23 - "Above all else, guard your heart, for everything you do flows from it."

Sin is more accessible today that it has ever been in the history of humanity. Our society sells sin to us through social media, ads, and entertainment. Everywhere you look is another temptation to overcome. It's plastered into our faces each day. If I'm being completely honest, I remember when I was just 7 years old my friend showed me inappropriate images on the internet. Let that sink in, 7 years old. He showed me on a computer and in todays culture and world pornographic material is just one click away.

Whether you are a male or female this is the silent killer of our generation and my heart breaks for the young people around the world who don't know what just one click can do to their future. So today, I implore you to think about what effect one click can have on your future. It is so much more than just watching one time. The enemy wants to trap you, but God's plan is for you to live free. Above all else, above what you see or feel tempted to do, guard you heart for everything you do flows out from that place.

Lord, help me to guard my heart against the plots of the enemy that seem to constantly be coming my way. Today, I choose to honor and obey you. I understand that just one click can lead to something much more dangerous. I receive your power to overcome. Amen.

Day 56:

Who you are is much more important than what you do.

Genesis 1:27 - "So God created mankind in his own image, in the image of God he created them; male and female he created them."

God created you in His image, plain and simple that is who you are. In today's society we are plagued and pressured to reach so many achievements. Our goals in life have become about the position, the title, and the clout. It can be so easy to place our identity in these things, but at the end of the day they will just leave you longing for more. God has created you to live from a place of identity in Him. This is where true happiness and content comes from! When you are known by Him, it is all you need to be known for.

Living from who He says you are is the only thing that will sustain you. Today, take time to think about who you are in Him and how beautiful it is that He would create you in His image.

Lord, thank you that I am that made your image. I no longer have to strive for a title, because the person you have created me to be is enough. I rest in the fact that I am created in your image and that is enough for me. I choose today to be confident and place my hope in you. Amen.

Day 57:

Submit to community, humility brings connection.

James 5:16 - "Therefore confess your sins to each other and pray for each other so that you may be healed."

Did you know one of the reasons God gave Adam his wife Eve was for community. God created us with the intention of being in deep fellowship with one another. I didn't always see the value in community and thought it was just for the more social people. Throughout my teenage years I found it hard to engage in meaningful church community. Many times I never made the effort to engage and because of that most of my battles I fought were fought alone. Community is vital to being encouraged in our walk with God. It gives us a place to be ourselves, to grow, to outwork the word with fellow believers, and a family to lean on in good and bad times.

Community is not just for the social butterflies, but it is the lifeline of our faith as believers. Community is who we are and how we were created to function. So today, make an effort to get involved and engage in your local church community.

Father, thank you that you created me for community. I no longer have to do this faith journey alone. Help me to humble myself and ask for help. I thank you that you've placed other believers in my life that are there to help me. Open my eyes to the power that is found in community. Amen.

Day 58:

Your calling is not about you.

John 15:16 - "You did not choose me, but I chose you and appointed you so that you might go and bear fruit — fruit that will last — and so that whatever you ask in my name the Father will give you."

This is a tough pill to swallow, but your calling is not about you. I remember being called to ministry at age 15 and walking by people thinking "they have no idea they just walked past the future pastor of a megachurch do they?" While it is so funny and childish now, how many times do we actually make our calling about us? We make it about how good our gift is or how much God is using us. While it's not bad to honor these things in your life, when the gift gets more attention than the One who gave it there is a problem. Your calling is about the broken, the hurt, and the lost.

When you get a revelation of that, God will grip you with such a burden for others it will be impossible to see injustice and not run to it with the name of Jesus! If you can learn to take yourself out the equation God will add things to your life! He wants to use you to reach the world for Jesus and to bear lasting fruit! Our calling is about the gospel being spread, it has nothing to do with our fame, success, or popularity! God has called you to be a builder of people not a builder of your platform. So today, take a moment to refocus yourself on why and what God has called you to do!

Lord, thank you that you have placed a great calling on my life. Humble me and help me to realize that my calling has nothing to do with me. The only part I play in this is my yes, but you are the one who gave me the gifts, the favor, the anointing, and the vision. Help me to focus my time on bearing fruit that lasts. Amen.

Day 59:

Take time to enjoy the word of God.

Psalm 1:1-4 - "Blessed is the man who does not walk in the counsel of the wicked, or set foot on the path of sinners, or sit in the seat of mockers. But his delight is in the law of the LORD, and on His law he meditates day and night. He is like a tree planted by streams of water, yielding its fruit in season, whose leaf does not wither, and who prospers in all he does."

I have good news for you today. You don't have to exhaust yourself or feel this pressure to be your best you every time you open Scripture. It's okay to approach it tired, broken, hurt, and lonely. That's what it's there for and the devil will do everything in his power to keep you out, because he knows that's how we win! Though it is vital to our growth to analyze, contextualize , and study Scripture sometimes it's okay to just read it. Learn to enjoy God and to enjoy His word.

Many times it can be so easy to dismiss reading His word and receiving the power that comes from that because we feel like we have to have it all together. God isn't concerned about your performance. He just wants you to come. It's okay to just sit back and read sometimes. So today, take a little extra time to remove any pressure you feel and focusing on enjoying God's word for what it is.

Lord, help me today not to overcomplicate things. I thank you that I can have an honest and open relationship with you. You don't care about how perfect I am, just that I come . Thank you allowing me to enjoy your presence. I give you all of me. Amen.

Day 60:

You need the baptism of the Holy Spirit.

Acts 1:8 - "but you will receive power when the Holy Spirit has come upon you; and you shall be My witnesses both in Jerusalem, and in all Judea and Samaria, and even to the remotest part of the earth."

You need the baptism of the Holy Spirit in your life. This is different from water baptism and salvation. When you receive Christ the Holy Spirit comes to live inside of you, but you have to activate His power in your life by surrendering to Him and asking for the baptism of the Holy Spirit. I remember when I was 14 at a Jesus Culture concert and they called for people with asthma to be prayed for now, I didn't have asthma, but I began to pray so wildly. God then began to fill me with the Holy Spirit and I received the baptism that night.

No, I didn't speak in tongues or fidget on the ground like we think will happen. I just felt God like I never had before and I was changed from that day on. In the coming weeks I began to lay hands on students at my school and see them healed, I began to pray in tongues, and I began my journey in the prayer closet. The baptism of the Holy Spirit is essential for your walk with God, because it's an impartation of power. It will also bring joy, fire, the gifts of God, boldness, and tongues into your life. The power to overcome and grow in your faith is found in the Holy Spirit! Jesus said one who is greater is coming to help you and that is the Holy Spirit! There's no pressure , just let Him do what He wants to do and at the right time you will be filled with power by the Holy Spirit.

Holy Spirit I ask for your baptism today. I need your power. I surrender my life to you, fill me with tongues of fire and boldness like a lion. I receive your activation in my life. Thank you for filling me to overflow. Amen.

Day 61:

Labour for the favor.

Psalm 90:17 - "May the favor of the Lord our God rest on us; establish the work of our hands for us — yes, establish the work of our hands."

God wants to pour out favor on your life. If you are completely confused about what that means, it just means that God wants to give you great and uncommon success. This is no trick,, but it says in the Bible that favor is a real thing. Abraham had it, David had it, Jesus had it, and you can have it! You must work hard to see the favor of God on your life. It does not come easy nor is it given out to just anyone. There is such a weight and responsibility to having the favor of God come on your life. I've seen it on my life many times with opportunities, open doors, financial blessing, promotion, my relationships, and success in the workplace.

A closed door is also a sign of the favor of God. If you weren't walking in His favor and blessing you would've walked through whatever door was open and compromised your calling. Quit complaining and groaning about it and thank God for the miracle of His protective hand in your life! I love this scripture, because it doesn't say God will do all the work for us or that He make it easy, but rather it says may He establish the work of our hands. This means we have to first work and then God can provide favor for us. I can't tell you how hard I've worked in life for the Kingdom and not seen His favor for seasons, it takes time! If we want the favor of God on our lives we have to understand that it comes from hard work and faithfulness. He has to know He can trust you with the spotlight. So today, take some time to declare HIs favor over your life and commit to working hard!

Lord, I declare your supernatural favor over my life. I ask that you would open doors that need opening and shut doors that need to be shut.

Day 62:

Don't remember you; remember Him.

Psalm 103:2 - "Praise the LORD, my soul, and forget not all His benefits."

I remember the first Hillsong service I ever attended. It was the end of January and I was just beginning a live out a dream of mine that had taken 6 years to come to pass. They took communion that day and the service pastor said something I will never forget. This is what he said: "don't remember you; remember Him." He continued by saying that we focus so much on our mistakes, our past, and our failures, but Christ didn't die for us to be stuck on these things. He then talked about how we should be remembering what He did for us, how He died for us, how He won our victory on the cross, and how good He has been to us.

Psalms reminds us to forget not His benefits. The benefits of life, of joy, of peace, and of every good thing. See, when we begin to remember what He did for us it activates our mind, soul, and spirit to focus solely on these things alone. The more we focus on His power the smaller our problems and past become. So today, I encourage you to reflect on what He has done for you and forget not His benefits!

Lord, today I forget not all your benefits. Thank you for dying for me on that cross so I wouldn't have to remember me, but so I could remember you and have a new life. Fix my eyes on your finished work Jesus. I thank you again for your salvation. Today I am moving forward and I now have new life in you. Amen.

Day 63:

Don't despise the pain.

Psalm 30:5 - "Weeping may endure for a night, but joy comes in the morning."

For those of you reading this right now I don't know your story. I don't know who cut you. I don't know how deep the cut is. I don't know how big the scar they left is. What I do know is that God wants to take that pain away from you. In season 3 of Stranger Things there's a monologue at the end where Officer Hopper is talking to El telling her to embrace the pain, because it means you are "out of the cave." Life is hard no doubt and you will be hurt, but don't despise the pain. God is a God or "re," He can revive your story, renew your heart, and restart your life. He wants to take the pain you've experienced and use it to bring others through. I know it hurts.

I know it sucks. Give to God and He will use you to impact others. Your test can become your testimony and your history can become part of His-story. Today, take time if you need to, to cry it out. God isn't afraid of the broken you, in fact He loves the broken you. He is the ultimate master of piecing things back together. You can trust Him with the pain you've been holding inside all these years. I believe God is calling you back home to Him! Smile, because pain may endure for the night, but joy is coming in the morning.

Lord I give you my pain today. I admit that I am so broken inside. I don't even know where to start, but I trust that you are my Healer. I give you permission to turn my test into my testimony. I know you restore all things so I'm believing you to restore all things in me. I declare that joy is coming my way. Amen.

Day 64:

Do you have a 'just a touch' mentality?

Luke 8:43-48 - And a woman was there who had been subject to bleeding for twelve years, but no one could heal her. She came up behind him and touched the edge of his cloak, and immediately her bleeding stopped. "Who touched me?" Jesus asked. When they all denied it, Peter said, "Master, the people are crowding and pressing against you." But Jesus said, "Someone touched me; I know that power has gone out from me." Then the woman, seeing that she could not go unnoticed, came trembling and fell at his feet. In the presence of all the people, she told why she had touched him and how she had been instantly healed. Then he said to her, "Daughter, your faith has healed you. Go in peace."

This is one of my favorite stories in the Bible of all time. This woman has inspired me beyond what words can express. I want to stir you today to move closer to Jesus with complete desperation.

129

This woman had been bleeding for 12 years. She had every reason in the world to give up, to be angry with God, and to lose all faith. Rather instead of losing hope she had a 'just a touch' mental ity. A broken, bleeding, and weak woman broke through the crowds of people with all she had left. When doctors said no, when people had forgotten her, and when all hope looked lost still she knew just one touch from Jesus would change everything
. I wonder what kind of miracles and breakthrough would happen in your life if you had that kind of faith and desperation. If we had the desire to push through obstacles and trials just to get a touch of Him. Just one touch is enough to move mountains. He can change everything in an instant if you'd just get hungry enough to be desperate for Him.

Jesus, you are my one pursuit in this life. Help me to have a mentality that chooses you over everything. I thank you that there is enough power in who you are to shift even the most impossible situations. Amen.

Day 65:

How's your self-talk?

Proverbs 16:24 - "Gracious words are a honeycomb, sweet to the soul and healing to the bones. "

Whether or not you realize it you are always talking to yourself. Each thought we have throughout the day is an inner dialogue. This can either be a really good thing or a really bad thing for you and it begs the question: how's your self-talk? Whether it's a decision like what coffee to get or what pants to wear or more serious things concerning self-worth and competence. It is so important to start rewiring your brain to think positive thoughts about yourself and your future . You'll realize that as you do this people will begin to be attracted to you, doors will open, and you'll feel better.

Positive self-talk also allows you to have more individual expression, better exercise habits, and you'll more easily recognize the negative thoughts and change them for good! God hasn't given you a spirit of fear but of a sound mind. He has called you to confidence and greatness! Good self-talk isn't prideful, good self-talk is respecting the sacrifice Christ made for you. He has given you a promise of an abundant life, but it starts with positive self-talk! So today, focus on talking positively to yourself and really embracing who God has created you to be.

Lord, thank you that you created me for confidence and identity. Help me to identify harmful self-talk. I declare life over myself today. Give me the courage and patience to speak positively to myself. Amen.

Day 66:

Purity is about asking God: "What do you want?"

Matthew 5:8 - "Blessed are the pure in heart for they will see God."

Today we are going to bust a myth. Purity is not just about sex or what you do with your physical self. Purity is much bigger than that and encompasses so many things we never touch on. See, being pure starts with your thoughts, motives, and desires. If you can learn to control those you will live a life pure and pleasing to the Lord. Purity is less about 'not doing something' and more about 'doing what God wants.' When we begin to focus on His desires and His actions then we naturally begin to look more like Him. God is the absolute embodiment of purity and whenever we follow in His ways we too are made pure.

I don't know about you, but I long to see God for who He is! Scripture says that if we become pure in heart we will see God. So today, focus on being obedient and taking His ways into consideration. Watch your thought life, relationships, and ideas about purity shift as you draw near to Him. You will begin to see and know Him in a deeper way than ever before.

Lord, I want to be a pure vessel for you. Help me to focus on obeying you. I commit myself to following you Lord. Open my eyes to see you in a new way. Amen.

Day 67:

God is your shield!

Psalms 3:1-6 - "Lord, how many are my foes! How many rise up against me! Many are saying of me, "God will not deliver him." But you, Lord, are a shield around me, my glory, the One who lifts my head high, I call out to the Lord, and he answers me from his holy mountain. I lie down and sleep; I wake again, because the Lord sustains me. I will not fear though tens of thousands assail me on every side."

In life we will all face attacks, not just battles, but attacks. The answer to the opposition you face is to know that God is your shield. When you get behind a shield you are taking refuge and we need not forget that God is our refuge. It's like a war bunker, when it's attack after attack, sometimes you just have to bunker down. God's presence is our war bunker and we can take refuge in Him.

Trust that He will see you through and He will lift your head, but it starts with taking refuge in Him. So how do we take refuge in Him? It's all about heart posture! In verse four David says he cried out to the Lord and the Lord answered Him. David had a posture of crying out to God. He wasn't angry or distant. Many times our first response is to get closed off and angry at God or people, but in reality, God always calls us to have a surrendered heart. Whether that's taking time to be in the secret place, declaring scripture, or holding back against your enemy. Whatever a surrendered heart posture looks like for you; that's how you are called to live. When we truly have that heart posture we learn to take refuge in Him. Today, remember despite what attacks you are facing that God is your shield!

Lord, thank you that you are my shield. I take refuge in you today and trust you completely. I speak victory and comfort over my life today in the name of Jesus! Amen.

Day 68:

God's plan for your life is good!

Jeremiah 29:11 - "For I know the plans I have for you,"
declares the LORD, "plans to prosper you and not to
harm you, plans to give you hope and a future."

Monopoly, an age old classic game, if you've ever
played it before you know that the objective of
monopoly is to 'pass and go' and collect your
inheritance to get more properties and win the
game. One of the things that stops that from
happening is being sent to prison in the game.
Would you believe me if I told you our lives are
kind of like a game of monopoly? Hear me out,
God's plan for us is to consistently move forward
and receive our 'pass and go.' This is the inheritance
Jesus won for us such as miracles, blessing, healing,
hope, and a good future. Jesus came to Earth to
break the curse of sin thus giving us an inheritance
of healing and hope.

Here's the problem, many times we end up in this bad decision cycle called sin where we keep making choices that land us in prison. Those of us who know Jesus also tend to use grace as our 'get out of jail free' card, but grace was never given to us as a license to do as we please. God's grace is there for you to move on and receive all He has for you not to have an excuse to make decisions that keep you in bondage! So today, realize that God's plan for your life is good and everlasting. Don't allow the enemy to keep you in bondage any longer!

Lord, I'm sorry for trying to do things my own way. I thank you that your plans for my life are good! I thank you that you plan to give me hope and a future. I declare all these things in your name! Amen.

Day 69:

Be careful not to identify a 'lack of opportunity'
with a lack of anointing.

*Luke 4:18 - "The Spirit of the Lord is upon me, because
he has anointed me to proclaim good news to the poor."*

I remember from around age 14 to 18 no one gave
me an opportunity to preach or serve alongside
them. I was on fire for the Lord and would preach
every week at a student led club, but yet outside of
that there was a lack of opportunity. The devil will
try to convince you that just because others don't
see or value the gift God has placed on your life that
you aren't valuable or anointed. Do not give in to
the lie. You are anointed with or without the
spotlight. It could be evidence that you still have
things to work on! Just because you never get a
chance or haven't been 'discovered' yet doesn't
mean God hasn't anointed you.

I remember being 18 and just graduated high school and everything changed for me. I was invited to speak at the middle school bible club, the ninth grade academy club, the neighboring high school, mentors were placed in my life, and I got hired onto a church staff while still doing all the above! Did I suddenly get more anointed because opportunity started coming through? No, God just decided it was time to increase my influence. He wants to do the same thing for you, but it's all about His timing. The anointing comes from being with Him, not being in front of people. Don't get discouraged. God has still chosen you. God is still for you. God's hand of favor is still on you. Today, take some time and press in for His anointing! When the time is right He will use you to shape the nations!

Lord, thank you that I am anointed and appointed by you. Give me the patience to wait things out. You have anointed me to preach the gospel to the nations! Thank you for your perfect timing. Amen.

Day 70:

Nothing compares to His presence.

Psalm 16:11 - "You make known to me the path of life; in your presence there is fullness of joy; at your right hand are pleasures forevermore."

A few weeks ago I went to a LANY concert and it was my first non-worship concert so I didn't know what to expect. I came in expecting a rush and a sense of joy, yet two songs into the first opening act I couldn't help but feel nothing. It wasn't because the music wasn't good or because I wasn't having a good time, but in that moment God was nowhere to be felt. I realized just how unlike anything in the universe His presence truly is, how great He truly feels, and how it's not just some stigma or cliche but His presence is really, truly, the most satisfying thing you can ever encounter.

Then it hit me, for all those people, LANY was their high, their moment, yet it was so empty when it's all said and done. What an honor it is to know Him. We have unlimited have access to His presence. My prayer is that our hearts never stop burning for those who are desperately searching for an answer. My prayer is that we always run harder and faster than ever before carrying the message of the gospel to a searching generation. His presence is the only thing that can ever satisfy our soul. He is such a good Father. God is just waiting for us to turn around and see He's been there the whole time

Lord, may I never take your presence for granted. Help me to never try and fill the void in my life with anything but you. I welcome your presence even right now in this moment. Guide me today and be extra near me to me as I go. Amen.

Day 71:

"Learn to wash a persons feet until you know why they walk the way they do." - Bill Johnson

John 13:1-17 - "After that, he poured water into a basin and began to wash his disciples' feet, drying them with the towel that was wrapped around him. He came to Simon Peter, who said to him, "Lord, are you going to wash my feet?" Jesus replied, "You do not realize now what I am doing, but later you will understand."......
When he had finished washing their feet, he put on his clothes and returned to his place. "Do you understand what I have done for you?" he asked them. "You call me 'Teacher' and 'Lord,' and rightly so, for that is what I am. Now that I, your Lord and Teacher, have washed your feet, you also should wash one another's feet. I have set you an example that you should do as I have done for you.

Jesus has called each and every one of us to wash each others feet.

Regardless of what they have walked through it is our mission to serve others in this way. So often we allow our first impressions of people to guide how we love and treat them. We are called to love them unconditionally and serve them as if it was Jesus right there in front of us. Jesus always took the time to understand people. He never dismissed or gave up on others, even though He knew what they had walked through. Jesus never expected or asked to be served, rather He sought to serve others. If we want to see our world change we must learn to serve others this genuinely and deeply. So today, schedule a meeting or conversation with someone who you may have disregarded or prematurely judged and let God do a work in your life and their life!

Lord, help me not to give up on others or even judge them. I want to serve them as you served all of mankind. I surrender all my preconceived notions and commit to being a lover of all people. Amen.

Day 72:

Christianity is the call to be the first ones there and the last ones to leave.

Romans 12:9-13 - "Let love be genuine. Abhor what is evil; hold fast to what is good. Love one another with brotherly affection. Outdo one another in showing honor. Do not be slothful in zeal, be fervent in spirit, serve the Lord. Rejoice in hope, be patient in tribulation, be constant in prayer. Contribute to the needs of the saints and seek to show hospitality. Bless those who persecute you; bless and do not curse them. Rejoice with those who rejoice, weep with those who weep. Live in harmony with one another. Do not be haughty, but associate with the lowly. Never be wise in your own sight. Repay no one evil for evil, but give thought to do what is honorable in the sight of all. If possible, so far as it depends on you, live peaceably with all.

Beloved, never avenge yourselves, but leave it[i] to the wrath of God, for it is written, "Vengeance is mine, I will repay, says the Lord." To the contrary, "if your enemy is hungry, feed him; if he is thirsty, give him something to drink; for by so doing you will heap burning coals on his head." Do not be overcome by evil, but overcome evil with good."

As Christians we have a mandate to be the first to show up and the last to leave anything, anyone, and anywhere. If you have said yes to Jesus you have committed your life to being the first at church to help and the last to stay and clean up. You've committed to being the first one to show up when someone is going through a trial or an emergency. You've committed to being the last one to leave when all the rumors are passing by and even when it may cost you your reputation to be associated with someone.

You've committed to being the first to weep with those who are weeping and celebrate with those who are celebrating. This whole Jesus thing has never been about us, but about laying down our lives for others. There are eternities hanging in the balance of our yes to the call of Christianity. I challenge you to be the first to show honor for your parents, teachers, pastors, coaches, and bosses. Be the first to put an end to the gossip around you and the last to even think about saying anything bad about someone. Be the first to reach out and the last to leave. Be the first to say sorry to the person that hurt you and the last to give up on them. Today, remind yourself of what it really means to be a christian and think about how you can put this into practice.

Lord, give me the courage to be the first to respond and the love to be the last to leave. This laying down my life thing isn't easy, but if you did it for me I want to do it for others. Open my eyes to opportunities on how to do that. Thank you for giving the ultimate sacrifice to us in Jesus. Amen.

Day 73:

The little details produce the larger then life moments.

Zechariah 4:10 - "Do not despise these small beginnings, for the Lord rejoices to see the work begin, to see the plumb line in Zerubbabel's hand."

The big life moments make doing the little details worth it. For me, it's the 5:15am wake ups, the 25min walk in the freezing cold to church and the moments you push yourself to reach out of your comfort zone. It's giving your all in each service not fully getting to receive a weekend experience. It's taking care of the mundane tasks like holding the dirty towel bag for baptisms or sweeping clean the entire first throw rows on the floor of trash, pamphlets, brochures, and envelopes each week that lead to moments like these. The night before I sat down and wrote this I witnessed 50 of the most beautiful smiles I had ever seen.

I witnessed the tears of joy from broken prayers of loved ones. I witnessed lifetime of bondages break off. I witnessed little ones encounter Him and eternities change all because of baptisms. The little details lead to moments like at Hillsong conference where I ran into my friend Isaac for the second time ever. Isaac didn't grow up in Australia. Isaac moved here all alone with no friends. When God led me to Isaac he was sitting by himself near the top row of a 2,800 seat auditorium. What I thought was mundane and out of my comfort zone to go talk to this man meant everything to him. At conference he found me, smiled as big as he could, hugged me and asked for pictures together. The man who I had only met once was overflowing with joy to see me again all because the Lord cares about and works in the little details. During worship at church I usually take a moment to look around and just observe what God is doing.

I am so thankful to God for the beauty that His church is. How almost every day for six years I'd stare at a Hillsong College poster and pray, believe, and dream for moments like these. The beauty of recognizing the little details will lead to huge life moments. Don't ever think your unseen, unspoken, or unrecognized efforts for the Kingdom have no power. That is a lie from the enemy. Don't give up and don't grow weary. There are salvations , baptisms, Isaacs, miracles, and precious moments in God's presence that are found on the other side of the little details. Today, realize that the Lord rejoices in seeing the work begin.

Lord, help me to be a person of thats involved in the little details. Thank you that I am seen and valued even if what I'm doing seems insignificant. Help me to see the power in doing the little things. I'm so grateful I get to serve you everyday. Amen.

Day 74:

Our obedience to Him is a direct response to our revelation of His love for us.

Jeremiah 7:21-23 - "This is what the Lord All-Powerful, the God of Israel, says: 'Go and offer as many burnt offerings and sacrifices as you want. Eat the meat of those sacrifices yourselves. I brought your ancestors out of Egypt. I spoke to them, but I did not give them any commands about burnt offerings and sacrifices. I only gave them this command: 'Obey me and I will be your God, and you will be my people. Do all that I command, and good things will happen to you."

Sadly, we have become a generation that is not very good at obeying God. We are okay with 'sacrificing' our Sunday mornings or 'sacrificing' swearing and think that is enough to please Him. While God loves to see you grow and give up things, He would much rather obedience from you in the first place.

If you have a little revelation of His love for you, you will desire to obey little. If you have a medium revelation of His love for you, you will be inclined/ desire to obey more. But if you understand, ponder, thank, and constantly receive what He did for you. Your only response is obedience. He took beatings and torture for you. He took the pain the pain of the cross and the guilt of all of humanity all out of love. This is why it is worth to obey Him, because it's never a sacrifice but always a completely honor to obey Him! When you feel like it's so hard to obey God, go into His presence and receive a revelation of His love for you. Your automatic response to a love that high, deep, and wide can only be what makes that person happy. You will want to do what honors them and be obedient to what they are asking. So today, ask yourself: What are some areas in my life that I need to be obedient in?

Father, I come to you today asking for forgiveness Help me to be obedient to you. I receive a deeper revelation of your love for me right now. Amen.

Day 75:

The wrong mindset about your past, present, and future can keep you from moving forward.

Phillipians 4:6-7 - "Be anxious for nothing, but in everything by prayer and supplication, with thanksgiving, let your requests be made known to God; 7 and the peace of God, which surpasses all understanding, will guard your hearts and minds through Christ Jesus."

There are three things in your life concerning time that can keep you from your destiny. These three things are the guilt of your past, the worry of your present, and the fear of your future. Let's deal with your past first. Quit punishing yourself over what Jesus already took the punishment for! My Bible tells me anyone who is in Christ is a new creation! My Bible tells me whom the Son has set free is indeed free!

The devil has no authority to keep you tied down any longer. Jesus finished it all on a tree called Calvary so you wouldn't have to live in guilt about the past! Now the worry of today is something that will haunt you if you let it. Scripture says be anxious for nothing, but take everything to prayer and God will hear you. Scripture gives us a promise of peace! It's okay to worry for a moment, but worry is not who you are! I believe even as you read this the God of your present is filling you with peace! Lastly, the fear of your future will cripple you greatly if you let it. Jesus said do not worry or be afraid of what tomorrow brings. God never said it would be easy, but He did give us a promise that He would never leave nor forsake us. Though you may be in a situation where you don't know what tomorrow looks like, I encourage you to put complete trust in God. If you will give the guilt of the past, the worry of your present, and the fear of your future to Him, He will give you peace and provision beyond what you even knew was possible.

Lord, I receive your forgiveness, peace, and provision. I don't have to worry about my past, present, or future, because I trust you completely. I rest in the finished work of the cross today. I am forgiven. I am secure. My tomorrow is in good hands. Amen.

Day 76:

Think about your ways.

Psalm 119:59-60 - "I thought about my ways and turned my steps back to Your decrees."

Self-reflection is a critical process in a believers life if we are to experience growth. We need to be okay with admitting our own faults and short comings. The only way to overcome a problem is to start by realizing you have a problem. We can't afford to fall asleep at the wheel of sin anymore. Psalms tells us to think about our ways. When we see how far off we have gone it will cause us to turn back to His way. What is your process of pulling out the weeds in your life? Do you ever internalize them? Do you write them down? Do you verbalize them with a trusted mentor?

One thing that could help is you finding that thing that needs improvement and searching the scriptures to see what God says about it! I hope we never lose the convictions of growth and seeking holiness. God still cares about having clean vessels. He still values holiness! So today, take some time to write out areas in your life where you could improve and back them up with Scripture.

Lord, thank you for giving me the Holy Spirit who allows me to recognize sin in my life. Help me to fill in Scripture where there is lack in my life. I surrender all my weak spots to you Jesus. Remind me throughout the day to take a moment with you and reflect on my actions. Amen.

Day 77:

Honor the past and embrace the future!

Phillipians 2:3 - "Do nothing out of selfish ambition or vain conceit. Rather, in humility value others above yourselves."

A wise friend of mine once told me to remember those in my life who have inspired my faith journey. I think honor is one of the most important values to have if you want to step into the promises of God for your life. There is just something special about honoring those who have gone before you and those who are currently inspiring you. Think about those in your life who have impacted you dearly and give them a call or even go the extra mile and so something for them. This wise friend of mine also told me to embrace the future by doing the same thing for others behind me. Someone in your life is looking to you for inspiration.

You have a choice to embrace the future or let the old flames die out. God is a generational God and calls us to value others above ourselves at all times. We do this by honoring those before us and making a difference in the lives behind us. Today, take some time and think about who you need to honor and who in your life you can impact for the cause of Christ.

Lord, give me a heart that honors others with everything that I have. Help me to be grateful and generous with my words and actions. Thank you that you are a multigenerational God. I commit my life to honoring the past and embracing the future. Amen.

Day 78:

Put on the garment of praise!

Isaiah 61:3 - "and provide for those who grieve in Zion — to bestow on them a crown of beauty instead of ashes, the oil of joy instead of mourning, and a garment of praise instead of a spirit of heaviness They will be called oaks of righteousness, a planting of the Lord for the display of his splendor."

As I was sitting here asking God what He wanted to say today I heard Him tell me to talk about putting on the "garment of praise." Now I've always heard about this but never really understood what it was about. If you are unfamiliar with the term garment it is just an article of clothing you put on to cover yourself. While it's pretty obvious we wear clothes to cover ourselves, we can do the same thing with our praise. The Bible teaches that praise is a weapon against our enemies.

This Scripture even says a garment of praise is to be worn in place of heaviness. Did you know you can praise off heaviness? Did you know when you're in a season of doubt, worry, and depression that putting on praise can shift your life? Praise is so powerful because it reminds us of who God is and what He has already done! Praise also reminds the devil that he has already lost. No demon in hell or on earth can stop you from praising! There is no demon that can keep its hold on you when you put on a garment of praise. A garment of praise will cover you! When you've messed up and feel exposed put on a garment of praise and the blood of Jesus covers all sin! So today, take a little extra time to put on a garment of praise!

Lord, I praise you for your wonderful works. Today I choose to put on the garment of praise. I declare that your praise will ever be on my lips! No more shall heaviness and depression plague my life, but you oh God, my source, you will be my strength! Amen.

Day 79:

Lament is a powerful weapon.

Psalm 102:1-2 - "Hear my prayer, O LORD! And let my cry for help come to You. Do not hide Your face from me in the day of my distress; Incline Your ear to me; In the day when I call answer me quickly."

You can be real with God. He doesn't want a fake version of you. Part of really understanding the Father's heart is knowing you can yell, be angry, and be broken before Him. As a loving Father He has given us the freedom to express how we feel. He actually gets glory out of us lamenting or telling Him what is really going on. If you're unfamiliar with what a lament is, it's just a passionate expression of grief or sorrow. We find these many times throughout the Bible. King David wrote many laments to express how he was feeling and what he was going through.

I remember my first semester of Hillsong College I was really battling my singleness. It's not that I so badly wanted a relationship or was seeking one out, but I just have this deep desire to love someone and build a God glorying future with that person. Anyways, I was battling with this and decided to write a lament. Now, I had never written a lament before, because I never really knew that was an option. I was able to freely express how I felt and how hard it really was before a God who actually cares and listens. I remember after writing this I felt so free and loved by Him. Writing a lament allows us to let go of the tough things! The only thing that you can ever give God that He can't already give Himself is your pain and brokenness. So today, if you are in a valley take time to write and pray out a lament. You can be brutally honest with God.

Lord, life is tough right now. I don't see a way out. I'm tired, broken, and beatdown. I know you are for me and all this will change soon. I'm believing for complete turnaround in Jesus name! Amen.

Day 80:

Do you have a creative outlet?

1 Peter 4:10 - "Each of you should use whatever gift you have received to serve others, as faithful stewards of God's grace in its various forms"

God has given you a gift. A gift that is meant to be used to influence others and serve His Kingdom. God has placed creativity in you. Because God created us in His image that means that creativity is a part of who we are. I used to think I was not creative at all and just meant to be a boring old normal preacher. As I grew in my faith and began to discover the gifts inside of me I began to find creative outlets that helped expressed what He is doing in me. One of these is creating graphics for social media. I've found it become a hobby, joy, and creative expression of who God is in me. Another one of these outlets is my sermons.

God wants to speak dynamically and creatively to others and I take great joy in crafting messages that are relevant to who I am sharing with. Lastly, I love taking pictures that make people feel a sense of awe or wonder. So my question for you today is do you have a creative outlet? God loves when His people express the gospel in ways that reach today's culture. We are called to get out of the box, but stay in the book. There is something so powerful about expressing outwardly what God is doing inwardly. Today, try to identify some of the gifts God has given you and how you can be creative with these to put Him on display!

Lord, thank you for giving me creative gifts and talents. Help me to discover those gifts and use them for your glory. You get all the glory out of this! Amen.

Day 81:

Becoming lukewarm will destroy your walk
with God.

*Revelation 3:14-16 - "To the angel of the church in
Laodicea write: These are the words of the Amen, the
faithful and true witness, the ruler of God's creation. I
know your deeds, that you are neither cold nor hot. I wish
you were either one or the other! So, because you are
lukewarm – neither hot nor cold – I am about to spit you
out of my mouth."*

When was the last time you were genuinely on fire
for God? I'm not talking about just lifting your
hands or being at every service, I mean when was
the last time you were on your knees crying out for
His Spirit? I think one of the biggest weapons the
enemy has used in today's Church is a spirit of
lukewarmness. We have gotten complacent with our
passion, our convictions, and our burden to reach
the lost.

God has called you to a life of passion and excitement in Him. We need not grow insensitive to His presence or His voice. If we aren't careful we can become lukewarm and lose the knowledge of understanding right from wrong. All you have to do to get your passion back is ask God and start doing! Pray again, fast again, move again, reach out again, and do whatever you need to do to get back on fire for Him! God is ready, willing, and able, but you have to make the first move! God desires to fill you until you overflow! Today, take a moment and ask God to fill you with passion again and start pursuing Him like it's the last day you'll ever have to do so!

Lord, I'm sorry for becoming lukewarm. I know at one point I was so on fire for you and your things. I repent of losing my sensitivity to you. I ask that you wouldn't just renew me, but that you would give me a new fire. I lay down my own desires to pick up yours. I receive your Spirit today that will cause overflow in my life! Amen.

Day 82:

If God seems silent, it's because the promise is on the way!

Philippians 2:5-11 - "In your relationships with one another, have the same mindset as Christ Jesus: Who, being in very nature God, did not consider equality with God something to be used to his own advantage; rather, he made himself nothing by taking the very nature of a servant, being made in human likeness. And being found in appearance as a man, he humbled himself by becoming obedient to death — even death on a cross! Therefore God exalted him to the highest place and gave him the name that is above every name, that at the name of Jesus every knee should bow, in heaven and on earth and under the earth, and every tongue acknowledge that Jesus Christ is Lord, to the glory of God the Father."

In the Bible God was silent for 400 years during the time between the Old Testament and New Testament. God did not speak to the Jewish people once during this period. The 400 years of silence began with the warning that closed the Old Testament: "Behold, I am going to send you Elijah the prophet before the coming of the great and terrible day of the LORD. He will restore the hearts of the fathers to their children and the hearts of the children to their fathers, so that I will not come and smite the land with a curse" and this silence period ended with the coming of John the Baptist, the Messiah's forerunner. After John the Baptist came Jesus, our Messiah and Savior. Now, to those living in this period of silence all hope seemed lost, I mean where was God? Even though they had completely turned their backs on Him I imagine some were still wondering where He was. What they didn't know is that during the silence the ultimate promise of Jesus Christ was on the way.

What they didn't know was that healing, deliverance, blessing, and a promise fulfilled were on the way. Maybe some of you reading this feel like God is silent, but it's only because His promise is on the way! Don't give up hope or lose sight of Him, because when God says He is going to fulfill a promise in your life it will come to pass! Today, just hang on a little longer for the promise is on the way!

Lord, speak to me today. Open up my ears and fill my life with your Spirit! I need your promise and voice in my life to come through. I trust that you have my best interest in mind. Thank you for who you are and what you are going to do. Amen.

Day 83:

God is a patient God.

2nd Peter 3:15 - "Also, regard the patience of our Lord as an opportunity for salvation, just as our dear brother Paul has written to you according to the wisdom given to him."

The other day I was thinking about the grace of God and how short of that I had fallen. During this moment the Lord reminded me that He is actually so patient with us. I think so many times we focus on the grace, love, and mercy of God, but never really regard Him as a patient God. Now when most of hear the word patient we get this image of waiting in a grocery store line and not biting our tongue or remaining calm in a tense moment, but it is actually so much more than that! Websters Dictionary says that patience is actually "the power to suffer with fortitude" it also states that it is an "endurance of evils or wrongs."

This broke me as I began to realize that this is the God we serve. How God in His patience would rather suffer and endure our wrong doings towards Him than give up on us. It hit me that His patience towards us is a constant and continual invitation to receive His salvation. God in all of His patience and goodness withholds wrath and invites us to sit at His table. This is exactly what Jesus did for us. He had the power to suffer with fortitude on the cross. Jesus on the cross, being nailed to a tree said "Father forgive them, for they know not what they do." He has been so patient with us! He has long suffered so you can receive His invitation! In Romans there is a beautiful passage that talks about how God had every right to pour out His wrath and display His power over us, yet His patience kept Him from releasing His judgment. It tells of how His wrath was ready for destruction, but was withheld due to His patience which displays His glory and mercy. So today, if you are feeling overwhelmed by your own guilt and shame know that God is patient with you. He is continually offering you an invite to His table because of His patience for all mankind.

Lord, I thank you for your patience on my life. I know I have messed up and done some things I regret. I repent and fix my eyes to you. I'm so grateful you withheld the judgment I so deserve to offer me a seat at the table. Today and the rest of my days of my life I choose you! Thank you Jesus for enduring the cross for me. Amen!

Day 84:

Let the joy of your Lord be your strength.

Nehemiah 8:10- "Nehemiah said, 'Go and enjoy choice food and sweet drinks, and send some to those who have nothing prepared. This day is holy to our Lord. Do not grieve, for the joy of the Lord is your strength."

If you know Jesus, joy is yours. We have so many beat up and depressed christians these days. That is an attempt to rob you of your destiny from the enemy! The Bible says that the joy of the Lord is your strength and if the devil can take away your joy he knows you'll be weak. Despite what you were told about your life, you were not created to walk around with your head down and heart heavy while hating everything. No! God created you to be full of joy and life! He created you to be strong and mighty. His joy is your source of life! Joy is one of our most powerful weapons against the attacks of the enemy!

He will try to rob you of your joy daily! When you feel the attacks coming declare that the joy of the Lord is your strength and watch things that used to tear you down just bounce off you. The joy of the Lord is the most amazing thing we could ever feel or encounter. We serve a happy God who wants to give us true and lasting joy! No longer do you have to go from binging shows, to being stuck in relationships, to lustful habits to try and find joy. Christ won that battle for you thousands of years ago! Today, take a moment and receive the joy of the Lord! I'm believing right now that in the name of Jesus chains of depression, anxiety, and addiction will be broken and the joy of the Lord will be your strength! Don't allow the enemy to label the spirit of depression as a mental illness, you have all authority on heaven and earth to cast out that spirit! You are an overcomer! Receive His joy today!

Romans 15:13 prayer - "May the God of hope fill you with all joy and peace as you trust in him, so that you may overflow with hope by the power of the Holy Spirit." Lord, I believe right now that your hope and joy is filling me. Depression and anxiety are no longer my portion, but I have a full and healthy life because of you Jesus! Amen.

Day 85:

Jesus is coming back!

Romans 14:7-9 - "For none of us lives to himself, and no one dies to himself. If we live, we live for the Lord; and if we die, we die for the Lord. Therefore, whether we live or die, we belong to the Lord. Christ died and came to life for this: that He might rule over both the dead and the living."

Jesus is coming back! This should be the best news you have heard all week! Jesus not only came, died, and returned to Heaven, but at some point He is coming back for us! There are three parts to Jesus being the Messiah. There is the death for our sins, the resurrection which tore the veil, and His return which will bring redemption for us and judgment for all sin. We tend to only live from two of these places. This means we miss out on the fullness of Jesus almost our whole lives.

We live from the perspective that He died and rose again, but we don't live from the perspective that He is actually coming back. When we get a revelation of that we should be completely changed in how we live. It should change our thoughts, actions, pursuits, and how we treat others. When we live from a place of knowing that He is coming back it changes our urgency to reach the world with the gospel. He is coming back to bring judgement on all sin! It is imperative we begin to reach others with the gospel so that He can truly reign over the living and the dead. Also, when we live from this perspective, each day is filled with joy and anticipation to finally see Jesus. We know that He hasn't left us here forever, but that one day soon we will see Him face to face. We should be living with an eager expectation to see Him! This should bring us joy and gratitude because soon we will with Jesus and our Father. So today, don't just live from a place of the death and ressurection, but realize that Jesus is coming back soon! Live with an urgency to save others and with a joy that He is soon returning!

179

Lord, help me to live with your return in mind! I don't want to just rest in what you have already done. Give me a burden for the lost and an excitement for your return! I long for the day I will see you face to face. Amen!

Day 86:

Give the devil no opportunity to come in!

2 Corinthians 6:3-4 - "We give no opportunity for stumbling to anyone, so that the ministry will not be blamed. But as God's ministers, we commend ourselves in everything."

The enemy will go through any crack in the door you leave open. The Bible says that the devil roams around like a lion looking for whom he can devour. We have a real enemy who wants nothing but to cause us to stumble. He wants to destroy your life so the reputation of the Father would be ruined . God calls us to live in such a way that there is not even a chance to stumble so the ministry cannot be blamed. This is why boundaries are so important to establish and set. Boundaries are not there to stop you from enjoying life they are there to protect you. Never put yourself in a situation where your faith could be compromised or tested!

If you have to get an internet blocking software do it, if you have to only hang out with your boyfriend/girlfriend in groups do it, it isn't worth losing the reputation of the Father! It takes a lifetime to build a good reputation, but only a second to ruin it. We must be wise with the choices we make and the people we are around. Our choices still have consequences! So today, what are some boundaries you need to set in your life?

Lord, give me wisdom in all situations. Make it apparent to me when I'm overstepping a boundary and giving the devil room in my life. Help me to live a life that is worthy of being attached to your name! Amen.

Day 87:

Generosity isn't about an amount; it's about the heart.

2 Corinthians 9:6-7 - "Remember this: The person who sows sparingly will also reap sparingly, and the person who sows generously will also reap generously. Each person should do as he has decided in his heart – not reluctantly or out of necessity, for God loves a cheerful giver."

I remember being eighteen and I had just gotten my first job at Dollar General. I really loved the Lord, but was in a season where I wanted to hold on to my money. The Lord kept telling me to give in the offering and to tithe 10% of my paycheck, but I was so reluctant. I knew the power, value, and impact it had, but I was just being stubborn. About two weeks after the Lord repeatedly told me to give (almost every day I was convicted) my car started having problems.

In a span of the next two weeks I would have two major repairs necessary in my car and I got a speeding ticket. Now, for most of you this would be coincidence, but for me I knew it was God giving me a nudge to get my finances in the right place. So, from then on I began to tithe every week for the right reasons and my life began to change. I got a nice little raise, I started having more success at work, and the favor of God started to fill my life. My point is that God desires for you to live generously with your finances. He isn't concerned with the amount, but the heart of which you do it with. We get so caught up in comparing our giving or think the impact lies in how much we were able to give. God promises that when we sow generously we will reap generously and I don't know about you but I want a God who is generous to my life! So today, realize that the amount you give doesn't matter as long as it is generous and done with the right intention!

Lord, help me to be a generous person. I want withhold nothing from you when it comes to my finances. Help me to trust that you will provide and protect me when I give. Thank you for the impact it will have on others. Amen.

Day 88:

Do people glorify God due to how you live?

Galatians 1:22-24 - "I remained personally unknown to the Judean churches in Christ; they simply kept hearing: 'He who formerly persecuted us now preaches the faith he once tried to destroy." And they glorified God because of me."

Are you living a life where people can look at you and glorify God? Are you kind to those around you? Do you have a generous spirit? Are you serving joyfully? Are you the same person outside of church as you are in church? I love this scripture because it says they didn't even know Saul, yet because of how he lived they glorified God! When people mention your name have you given them ammunition to shoot you down with or have you given them ammunition to praise God with?

Living right goes so much further than just ourselves! What an honor it is to hear people come up and say "Wow! Thank you for living so close to God, you've inspired me to know Him more." Just by your example you can change someones life! So remember, you may just be the only Jesus some people will ever see.

Lord, help me to realize my actions have consequences for others too. Thank you that I get to be an example to the world of you. May I never get any glory for loving you, but may others marvel and give glory to you for what you've done in my life. Amen!

Day 89:

God laughs at the impossible.

Ephesians 3:20-21 - "Now to him who is able to do immeasurably more than all we ask or imagine, according to his power that is at work within us, to him be glory in the church and in Christ Jesus throughout all generations, for ever and ever!"

What seems impossible to us is just a snap of the fingers for Him. He speaks and mountains move. He whispers and chains break. He blinks and the oceans roar. All authority to create and destroy is in every word He speaks. All God has to do is breathe and things obey. He is Lord over all creation. You may be on day 89 and still wondering why nothing has changed. The God is the impossible is coming your way and He has taken an entire day out of this book just to send you this message. We serve a King who walked on water and who healed at the snap of His fingers.

We serve a King who was the most dead you could possibly ever be and yet He rose from the dead. We serve a King who knows what it is like to be fully man and fully God. Don't think for one-second He doesn't know what you are going through! Lift your eyes today and see that the God of the impossible is coming your way!

Lord, you are a God of the impossible. What seems uncontrollable to me is in your complete control. Help me to focus my eyes on you in all seasons. Amen.

Day 90:

Your family matters too.

Acts 10:2 - "He and all his family were devout and God-fearing; he gave generously to those in need and prayed to God regularly."

I know some of you reading this might be in a stage of life where you don't see why family is so important. Maybe some of you reading this are going crazy because of your family. Maybe you are reading this and you never really had a solid family whether it was a parent missing or having to live with both parents at different times. Maybe you're reading this and you don't even talk to your family anymore because of what happened in the past. God's plan for the family unit is to live in unity so He can pour out His blessing from generation to generation. Since the beginning of time the devil has tried to split up families.

The devil knows that God passes on blessing and anointing through bloodlines. God desires for your family to live in unity, peace, love, and forgiveness. You may think the idea of family is outdated, but in fact it is His master plan to reveal the sacrificial love of Christ, the giving love of the Father, and the empowering love of the Holy Spirit. We are called to serve the Lord together as a household. So today, do whatever is in your power to restore what has been broken and watch God move in your family!

Lord, thank you for the blessing that is family. Help me to forgive where forgiveness is needed. Help me to swallow my pride and apologize where I need to. Even if I am the only one doing so I will fight for my family, because you fought for me. Thank you that family matters. I just declare blessing, favor, and protection over all my family in the name of Jesus! Thank you for restoration. Amen.

Day 91:

You can pray things into existence.

Phillipians 4:6 - "Do not be anxious about anything, but in every situation, by prayer and petition, with thanksgiving, present your requests to God."

Your prayers are powerful. Despite how you feel about your prayer life if you know God your prayers have an impact on the Earth. As sons and daughters of the King we can pray things into existence based off the authority God has given us. Even Jesus said ask anything in my name and it shall be done. I believe God is looking for intercessors all across the globe. If you have no idea what intercessory prayer is, it's basically just praying into the future. If you have ever prayed for someone to be healed or for something to happen you are interceding. Our prayers have the power to shift things into reality.

When you intentionally intercede you are praying into a moment on the timeline of history that has yet to happen. There is something so powerful about covering nations, yourself, your family, and believers in intercessory prayer. The Bible tells us that Jesus is sitting at the right hand of the Father interceding on our behalf. That just means Jesus is constantly day and night praying into your future and your life. You can pray healing into existence. You can pray revival into existence. You can pray salvations into existence. You can pray breakthrough into existence, because of Jesus! I remember one time when I intentionally started to intercede and I asked the Holy Spirit to take control of my prayer and as He did I began to pray and weep for a nation in Africa. I don't even remember what country it was, but I prayed for about fifteen minutes and was weeping and broken for that nation. I remember it was the craziest feeling I ever had, because it had nothing to do with me and everything to do with His Kingdom coming to Earth. When we understand the power of our prayers we shift the course of history. You are called to shift history with your prayers and petitions to the Father! So today, take time to intercede on behalf of your nation, your family, yourself, and anything you know needs prayer! Remember, you can pray things into existence!

Father, thank you that you hear my prayers. Thank you that my prayers have an impact in the course of history! Help me to pray the impossible down from heaven into reality on Earth. Amen!

Day 92:

A moment with God is never a moment wasted.

Psalm 16:11 - "You will make known to me the path of life; In Your presence is fullness of joy; In Your right hand there are pleasures forever."

A moment spent with God is never a moment wasted. In fact, being with Him is the most important and best use of your time you could ever have. When you spend time with Him you are investing into eternal things. I'm not sure about you, but I would much rather spend time storing up things that will last forever than to be striving for things here that will one day get left behind. God has so many things He wants to share with you, but you must first prioritize knowing Him. Being in His presence isn't some chore, serving isn't some have to, and saying no to sin isn't a wasted opportunity. We say we want to live in the moment, but we always mean our moment.

So we go party, sin on purpose, and try to live it up as if it's our last. I know this is hard to hear, but if you are not investing your time, effort, money, and life into the things of God you are wasting your time on Earth. I began to realize this from a young age and I remember almost every night for several years I would shut the door to my room and pray and worship. There were several times where I didn't go hang out with friends or go to sports games, because I want to be with Him. I remember I didn't go to homecoming or prom my entire high school time, because I didn't want to invest my time into things that would not have honored God. Now, I'm not saying if you go to prom or homecoming you are wasting your time or doing a bad thing, but I am saying there are seasons where God wants to draw you in. These were the best times of my life with God! I would pray, cry, laugh, witness miracles, praise with angels in my room, and its where physical manifestations of God's presence would come and shine on my hands.

As it did with Moses when He came down and His face shone due to the glory of the Lord! I tell you these things to encourage you that not one moment in God's presence is wasted. He will touch you, anoint you, and guide you when you learn to value His presence. So today, know that a moment spent with God is never a moment wasted.

Lord, I'm sorry for putting you second in my life when it comes ti what I invest my time in. Help me to put my life into perspective and realize that only eternal things truly matter. I want to spend my time honoring and loving you. I give you permission to come and touch my life again. Amen.

Day 93:

Someone needs you to stand in the gap for them.

Psalm 82:3-4 - "Defend the weak and the fatherless; uphold the cause of the poor and the oppressed. Rescue the weak and the needy; deliver them from the hand of the wicked."

When is the last time you stood up for someone? I don't mean just loved someone nor do I mean just comforted them. I'm asking you when is the last time you really truly stood in the gap for someone? When it actually cost you something? Scripture doesn't just suggest we defend the weak and fatherless or rescue the needy, it commands us to stand in the gap for them. As I sit here writing this teary eyed my heart breaks for every baby aborted, every woman or man raped, every person taken advantage of, every person suffering from depression, and anyone who has been so beaten down by life that they've lost their voice.

God demands that we be a voice for those who have no voice. That means you throw away your opinion and you pick up what the word of God says about the situation. His word is clear. You are called to stand in the gap and be a bridge to the Father's heart. So today, think about who you can you stand in the gap for? Jesus stood in the gap for you on that cross and beckons us to do the same!

Lord, give me the courage to stand in the gap for those who are helpless. Give me a voice to speak for those who have no voice. Give me compassion for those who are in dark places. I do not take lightly the fact that I am supposed to stand in the gap. I receive your boldness and wisdom to speak life and cause change. Amen.

Day 94:

Hey you! Dare to dream big!

1st Corinthians 2:9 - "But, as it is written, "What no eye has seen, nor ear heard, nor the heart of man imagined, what God has prepared for those who love him"

I can already tell you, you're thinking too small about your life. I do not care if you have the world's craziest most impossible dream, because Gd is on your side it still isn't big enough. God consistently calls you to dream the impossible and do it. Did you know God has nations for you? The Bible clearly states that God has a heart for nations and that He wants to give us influence in the nations of the Earth. I wonder if you can even see yourself in positions of great influence. Part of seeing what no eye has seen has to do with our own self-image. You will never go or be what you don't already see yourself as.

I will never be a leader if I don't see myself as a leader. I will never touch the nations if I don't see myself or believe that God wants to use me in that way. I don't know about you, but I long to see what is not even possible to comprehend. I want to inspire you to dream as crazy, big, and wild as God leads you to do. Don't settle anymore! It is time to start dreaming about influencing the nations of the Earth! Today, ask God first for a dream if you don't already have one and secondly ask Him to give you a specific nation. You will see your heart for people and for spreading the gospel change!

Lord, I declare that the nations are yours Lord and that you will use me to reach them with the gospel. Help me to see myself as blessed and highly favored. Thank you for using me to reach the one and using me to reach multitudes. Your plan for my life isn't small and insignificant, but it is huge and beyond anything I could ever comprehend. I can't wait to see all you do. Amen.

Day 95:

Don't eat it!

Proverbs 23:6 - "Do not eat the bread of a man who is stingy."

You can't always control what comes into your life, but you can control what you swallow and digest. You can spit anything out that doesn't have God written on it. How often do we 'eat the bread' of what others offer us? We take in stinginess, unforgiveness, anger, and whatever else comes our way. You should be eating the bread of life named Jesus! You are called to love all people, but that doesn't mean you have to roll around in the mud with them and get all dirty. Stinginess is one of the biggest barriers of blessing. If you do not release what is in your hands God can not bless you with what's in His. So today, refuse to take in just anything and get away from any sources of negativity in your life.

Lord, help me to see that I don't have to take in every little thing that comes my way, I receive a discerning spirit about what I need to keep and let go of in my life. I want only the things that glorify you. Amen.

Day 96:

The Church is the hope of the world.

Isaiah 2:10 - *"This is the message that was revealed to Isaiah son of Amoz concerning Judah and Jerusalem: In the last days the mountain of the house of the LORD will be established as the chief of the mountains; it will be raised above the hills, and all nations will stream to it. And many peoples will come and say: "Come, let us go up to the mountain of the LORD, to the house of the God of Jacob. He will teach us His ways so that we may walk in His paths." For the law will go forth from Zion, and the word of the LORD from Jerusalem. Then He will judge between the nations and arbitrate for many peoples. They will beat their swords into plowshares and their spears into pruning hooks. Nation will no longer take up the sword against nation, nor train anymore for war."*

The Church is a beautiful gathering of God's people and the means by which the purpose of Jesus can be fulfilled on the earth. No, I'm not just talking about a building, but rather a people who are alive and ready to shape eternity with the gospel. I love this scripture in Isaiah, because it gives us a beautiful image of what The Church should be modeling for the world. The Church should be established amongst the Earth. This means we should be known for having the greatest gifts, the most excellent work, the most loving people, and the most positive aspects of the world should be tied back to our name. Secondly, the nations should be streaming to The Church for answers and for purpose. Remember how we just talked about nations a couple of days ago? It is God's plan for The Church to influence and captivate the nations because of the message of Jesus Christ. Thirdly, people should be hungering for the Lord and longing to know His ways, because of the example The Church has set for them. This Scripture says others will say, not will be told to go to the house of the Lord, meaning that by seeings how The Church functions their eyes will be opened to the goodness who He is. Then it talks about how "they will beat their swords into plowshares and their spears into pruning hooks. Nation will no longer take up the sword against nation, nor train anymore for war." This is so beautiful, because The Church is supposed to cause peace in the nations. This includes the Syria's, Iraq's, and all the nations who seem to never cease fighting. God's plan for The Church is so beautiful and perfect that even those in places like China, Turkey, and those in groups like Isis will bow at His mighty name and repent. The Church has been purposed with being the perfect reflection of the Father. Now obviously we are not perfect, but when we move together in unity and are obsessed with seeing the glory of the Lord cover the world these things will happen! The house of the Lord will be established, the nations will stream to it, people will long for His commands, and peace will rule the earth!

Lord, today I declare that The Church will wake up from its slumber! I declare that The Church will be a place where the house of the Lord will be established, the nations will stream to it, people will long for His commands, and peace will rule the earth! I come against any more division and hate within the body. Devil you will not have your way any longer. The Church's greatest days are ahead in the name of Jesus! Revival is coming to all nations, tribes, and tongues! Amen.

Day 97:

If it's out of your control, it's not yours to worry about.

Exodus 14:14 - "The LORD himself will fight for you. You need only to be still"

Recently I was talking to a friend about a situation they were going through that was out of their control. The Lord spoke to me and I began to think about how so many times we carry around weight that isn't ours to carry. Yes, worry about things you can control, but it is so silly to stress yourself out over something that you absolutely cannot change. You cannot change someones mind or behavior for them. You are only able to control how you feel and how you react. Your need to control things will change when you realize who is fighting for you! Whatever you are facing that is out of your control is now the Lord's battle.

Scripture says the Lord Himself will fight for you, but you must stay still. That means stop fretting, worrying, and losing sleep over it and the Lord will handle it! Take a deep breath and understand that the God who has never once lost a battle is fighting yours! It takes the same amount of energy to sit there and worry as it does to fix your eyes on Jesus! He is good and He is fight ing for you! Today, focus on who He is and let go of what is keeping you up at night!

Lord, I believe even as I pray this you are fighting on my behalf. I release my doubts and worries to pick up your victory today. No longer will I worry about the things I cannot control. You are for me and no weapon formed against me shall prosper in the name of Jesus! Amen.

Day 98:

Serve with no expectation that you'll get something back.

Ephesians 6:6-8 - "Don't work only while being watched, in order to please men, but as slaves of Christ, do God's will from your heart. Serve with a good attitude, as to the Lord and not to men, knowing that whatever good each one does, slave or free, he will receive this back from the Lord."

What is your motive behind serving? Are you looking to be noticed or praised? Are you looking for a job opportunity or looking to spend more time with a certain person? If we aren't careful we will end up doing the right things for the wrong reasons. God has called us to serve others with no ulterior motives. We get so entangled in titles, praises, and promotion that we lose sight of why we actually give our lives to the call of Christ. Serving is never about you and never will be.

It is not about your talents or your abilities, but only about the heart of the Father being displayed. I know this may be a gut check for some of you, but God will do amazing things with your life if you serve Him with a good attitude that comes from your heart. Sure, others who are serving for the wrong reasons may be the first chosen or first noticed, but fruit from a sour tree doesn't last! If you want your life and service to the Lord to last make sure it is done with the right heart and mindset! So today, take the time to reevaluate why you are actually serving.

Lord, help me to reach the lost with how I serve. Help me to have no secret motives or expect anything back in return. I lay down my life for others and to see them encounter you. Remind me next time I serve of why I even do it. Amen.

Day 99:

God is completing a good work in you.

Phillipians 1:6 - "I am sure of this, that He who started a good work in you will carry it on to completion until the day of Christ Jesus"

Phillipians 1:9-11 - "And I pray this: that your love will keep on growing in knowledge and every kind of discernment, so that you can approve the things that are superior and can be pure and blameless in the day of Christ, filled with the fruit of righteousness that comes through Jesus Christ to the glory and praise of God."

Day 99, never did I imagine we would all make it here! If you've stuck it out and read through these devotions I am confident God has been completing a good work in you! This is both a statement of confirmation and a statement of hope. Maybe you are on day 99 and feel as if God has yet to do anything in your life.

I want to reassure you that God is completing a good work in you! He will complete His promise in your life. His plan is for you to grow in His love, knowledge, and discernment. He wants you to be filled with the fruits righteousness! This is the hope we have to hold on to even in the good and bad seasons that God is completing a good work in us. I just want to prophecy over someone that God isn't finished with your life yet. He hasn't forgotten you and He never will. Keep going strong and you will see the fruit of His good work in your life come to pass. I do not know who this is for, but you are not the only one who feels like giving up. It will get better, because God is causing all things to work in your favor! So today, don't give up and keep pushing forward, because God is completing a good work in you!

Lord, thank you for bringing breakthrough into my life. Stuck is not my destiny. I speak revival and renewal! I will grow in love, knowledge, and discernment. Amen!

Day 100:

Love God and love people.

Mark 12:30-31 - " Love the Lord your God with all your heart and with all your soul and with all your mind and with all your strength.' The second is this: 'Love your neighbor as yourself.' There is no commandment greater than these."

Wow! You made it! We are here on the last day and what a journey it has been. I can't even imagine the journey each one of you has been on! Everything this book talks about really comes down to two things: loving God and loving people with all your heart, mind, soul, and strength. If you learn to do those two things and learn what it looks like to live those out everything I've talked about the past 100 days will take place in your life. When we love God and love people we come more passionate for His presence, blessing, transformation, and glory.

When we love Him, worship becomes who we are and we long to see His Kingdom come to Earth. When we love people we will treat them well and be moved with compassion for them. We also long to reach out, stand in the gap, and serve them with no ulterior motives! So today, as we close out this journey, I encourage you to always love God and love people! Doing these two things will cause you to live on purpose.

Lord, help me to truly love you and your people with all I am. I want to get these two things right and I know once I do, you will fill in the gaps for me. Thank you for all this 100 days has done to bring us closer together. I love you and thank you for how you've changed me. Help me to keep and put into practice the things I've learned. Amen.

My prayer for you:

Lord, I ask that you would bless the reader. Use them for your glory Lord and bring deliverance in the name of Jesus! Return back to them ten times the portion which they have invested into your Kingdom! I believe in the name of Jesus that what they lost will be restored, that favor is coming their way, and that You God will use them mightily to reach the nations! May they never give up or fall away from seeking You. I close with this prayer from Numbers 6:24-26 - "May the Lord bless you and keep you; may the Lord make his face shine on you and be gracious to you; may the Lord turn his face toward you and give you peace." Amen.

About the author:

Caleb Gaines grew up in Louisiana until Hurricane Katrina forced him and his family to move to Alabama and then Georgia. Soon after moving to Georgia he would start attending Jentezen Franklin's church Free Chapel. At age 13 he got saved and at age 15 Caleb received the baptism of the Holy Spirit. Caleb then led a revival in his 8th grade year that saw many students healed and saved. During the summer of 8th grade going into 9th grade the Lord told Caleb to start a student led church called Standout Church which later changed names to Purpose Fellowship. Caleb pastored and led this fellowship for seven years as he mentored those below him to takeover once he moved. They saw hundreds if not a thousand students influenced, healed, saved, delivered, and transformed by the gospel.

He was also on preaching rotations at White County Middle school and 9th Grade Academy's Fellowship of Christian Athletes and Habersham County High School's FCA. Caleb has been preaching since the age of 13 and has spoken at Free Chapel Youth, Light Up The Nations Church, and The Bridge Church youth ministry as part of his internship. He is now officially an author at the age of twenty-one and loves all people. Caleb has aspirations to one day plant and pastor a multicampus church in Oakland, California full of conferences, influence, community outreach, God's presence, revival, and community. Caleb is currently living out his dream of studying pastoral leadership at Hillsong College in Sydney, Australia.

71278570R10133

Made in the USA
Columbia, SC
25 August 2019